SIGNIFICANT WORK

*Discover the Extraordinary Worth
of What You Do Every Day*

PAUL RUDE

**EVERYDAY
SIGNIFICANCE**

Unless otherwise indicated, all Scripture quotations are from The Holy Bible, English Standard Version® (ESV®), copyright © 2001 by Crossway, a publishing ministry of Good News Publishers. Used by permission. All rights reserved.

Scripture quotations marked NIV are taken from the Holy Bible, New International Version®, NIV®. Copyright © 1973, 1978, 1984, 2011 by Biblica, Inc.™ Used by permission of Zondervan. All rights reserved worldwide. www.zondervan.com.

Scripture quotations marked KJV are taken from the King James Version of the Bible.

Significant Work: Discover the Extraordinary Worth of What You Do Every Day
Published by Everyday Significance, Copper Center, Alaska.
www.EverydaySignificance.org
Cover design by Tribe+Mighty

ISBN: 978-1-939310-10-1 (hc)
ISBN: 978-1-939310-11-8 (ebk)
Library of Congress Control Number: 2012951218
Work—Religious aspects—Christianity
Work—Biblical teaching
Printed in the United States of America
10 9 8 7 6 5 4 3 2 1 PPC

To
my father,
Terry Rude,
who radiates an extraordinary passion for God's glory.

CONTENTS

INTRODUCTION

We've all heard the lie. It's the one that says people in full-time Christian ministry have a higher calling, a greater purpose, a more significant vocation—a more meaningful life—than people who work in secular jobs.

When we hear that lie from seminar speakers, our well-meaning friends, and other people we respect, we can't help but wonder if it might be true. We begin to question if all the exhausting effort—the daily grind of our lives—makes any lasting difference in the grand scheme of things. And then an accusation hits us. It comes in the form of a question: Are we wasting our lives in work that doesn't count for eternity?

Our heads hit the pillow, and in the fleeting seconds before we blink out another nameless day, a vague, hollow feeling gnaws at us—a sense that our life's work won't leave the tiniest of fingerprints on the shape of eternity. Not even a smudge. After all, as kids in Sunday school, we learned that only what's done for Jesus will last. (And that clearly meant praying, witnessing, giving money, or—most glorious of all—surrendering to the call of full-time Christian ministry.) The teacher told us that everything else we do in life will burn up in blazing flames and smoke when Jesus returns and annihilates the earth.

I certainly wasn't the brightest little kid in the class, but as we all sat there in wide-eyed terror, I thought, *Dang. Grown-up life sure seems like a lot of hard work just to see it all go up in blazes and smoke.* But who's to question the Sunday school teacher? So we charged out of class and into life with the bewildering notion that a chosen few would get the call to ministry—the call to a life of significance. Meanwhile, the rest of us poor schmucks would work like crazy on bulldozers, computers, aircraft engines, and a bunch of other stuff that was totally insignificant to God. In fact, it would all just burn up someday. Bummer.

But it's a lie—that accusation, that hollow sense, that bewildering notion that secular work has no lasting value. It's the lie of *vocational guilt.* And it subtly devalues the lives of millions of CPAs, auto technicians, MBAs, homemakers, retail associates—people just like you and me. The goal of this book is to shatter that lie. Let's start by defining it; we need a clear target in our crosshairs.

---

vocational guilt |vō'kā sH ənl| |gilt|

noun [noun phrase]

- a sense that our work and daily toil make no lasting difference in eternity
- a feeling of having failed to do something meaningful with one's life
- the fear of inaccurately discerning one's life calling (or vocation)
- the frustration or discouragement endured by laypersons who believe that only Christian ministry (church work, evangelism, relief work, etc.) is significant to God

---

Before diving into the following pages, we need to clarify a few preliminary concepts; otherwise we might get our signals crossed. First, our *vocation* encompasses far more than just our paid work. It includes our paid work, but our vocation also encompasses all the unpaid work, activities, and relationships of life. For example, my wife, Misty—mother of five energetic kids, keeper of one undomesticated husband, manager of a vibrant household—technically doesn't have a paying job, but she certainly has a vocation.

Second, our *calling,* like our vocation, encompasses far more than just the work we do. There are two aspects to our calling: our *primary* calling and our *particular* calling. Our calling is first and foremost the call to trust and follow Jesus Christ—this is our *primary* calling. But as we follow him, he leads us into the particular spheres, or aspects, of our unique lives—these spheres constitute our *particular* calling. One of those many spheres is the specific work we do. Understood biblically, our vocation and calling are one and the same; they encompass all of life.

Third, when referring to non-religious work, or the work we traditionally define as secular, I prefer to use the term *marketplace* work rather than *secular* work. The term *secular,* by definition, carries the implication of having no eternal value. For the follower of Jesus Christ, however, every moment and every aspect of life is infused with extraordinary eternal value, so nothing is truly secular in the strict sense of the term. Jesus Christ is Lord of all seven days of the week, not just Sunday.

Finally, this book is not a how-to book. If you're looking for a step-by-step guide to discovering the specific career path you should choose, then you have the wrong book in your hands. Shoot me a note through our website, *www.EverydaySignificance.org,* and I'll send you some recommendations for good books on career guidance. However, if you want to discover the astonishing significance of the work and other tasks you're already doing—if you want to see why your vocation is spectacularly meaningful in God's eyes and why it makes a lasting difference in eternity—then keep reading.

The truth is stunning. The truth is that the regular, everyday, earthly work of our lives holds a breathtaking significance bestowed by the touch of God's magnificent glory alone. The daily grind of our lives leaves far more than a tiny fingerprint on eternity. It strikes cosmic hammer-blows that forge the very shape of eternity.

God pulls the white-hot ingot of eternity from the forging fire of his sovereignty. Then, like master to apprentice, he entrusts the hammer to our hands. He says, "Strike it. Strike it right here. This is your place. This is where I want you to shape eternity. Live the life I gave you to live." And so, in stammering awe, we take up the hammer. We live our lives—our regular, everyday, toilsome lives. The hammer falls. Sparks fly. Eternity bends, and the Master is delighted.

God, the Maker of the universe, destines our everyday lives to make a difference that lasts forever? Yep. Fuel filters, tax returns, laundry, and southern-style barbecue are important to God? Yep (especially southern-style barbecue). A life as an engineer, florist, or realtor is as meaningful to God as the life of a pastor, missionary, or humanitarian relief worker? Absolutely.

If this is true, then why do so many of us continue to live with the basic assumption that ministry work and humanitarian work are more meaningful and important to God than marketplace work? In other words, if vocational guilt is a lie, then why do so many of us believe it?

In this book, you and I have a story to unfold. This story is really a battle—the battle between vocational guilt and truth. In Part One, we will uncover the lie of vocational guilt. We'll find it lurking in our churches, homes, and jobs. We'll see its devastating impact on our faith.

We'll also explore the three main reasons many of us still believe the lie. First, we've heard the lie for such a long time (2,300 years and counting) that it's become an embedded part of our culture. Second, the reality of life screams *futility*. After all, how *eternally significant* do you and I feel when we drag ourselves into the office, warehouse, or restaurant kitchen on Monday morning? Third, the dark heart of the lie is rooted in pride. In a twisted sneer, it proclaims, "*I* will authenticate *my* significance. *I* will prove *my* worth to God."

In Part Two, we'll put an end to vocational guilt. We'll shatter the lie with the everlasting truth of the Bible—the written Word of God. Never again will we doubt the significance of our daily work or of our lives. We'll discover that there's something massive going on here—the cosmic epic of God's story—and we're smack in the middle of it. He knows your name and mine. He's given us each a life to live—a regular, everyday life—a particular place for us to shape eternity.

You and I look at our ordinary lives and think, "Seriously? *That's* supposed to be epic?" But the Master delights in it. He forges his masterpiece with it. And when we see what he does with it, it will blow our minds. It will thrill the hearts of men, dazzle the angels, delight the heart of God, and glorify his name. Forever.

PART ONE

THE LIE

CHAPTER 1

THE QUESTION OF SIGNIFICANCE

It is inbred in us that we have to do exceptional things for God; but we have not. We have to be exceptional in the ordinary things.

—Oswald Chambers[1]

It would be a mistake to infer from the call to war-time living . . . that Christians should quit their jobs and go to "war"—say, to become missionaries or pastors or full-time relief workers. That would be a fundamental misunderstanding of where the war is being fought.

—John Piper[2]

---

[1] Oswald Chambers, *My Utmost for His Highest* (Uhrichsville, Ohio: Barbour and Company, 1987), 218.

[2] John Piper, *Don't Waste Your Life* (Wheaton, Illinois: Crossway, 2004), 131.

The interview playing over my car radio was standard fare. The host of a Christian program was interviewing a wildly popular contemporary Christian music star—little more than background noise as I drove down the highway. But then the discussion landed on the topic of serving the Lord in ministry. The music star told the listening world how his brother was once a truck driver but gave up trucking in order to serve the Lord as an assistant pastor. This drew hearty affirmation from the host, who was actually laughing at the comparative insignificance of truck driving. The music star then reflected on his congratulatory words to his brother: "I always thought you had more in you than being a trucker."

There are 3.2 million truck drivers in the United States.[3]

I turned the interview off and silently drove down the highway, wondering, *What are the truck drivers who heard that interview feeling right now?* A superstar Christian just implied that 3.2 million truck drivers are less significant than assistant pastors.

A massive question now hangs in the air—a question loaded with profound implications for the significance of *your* life and vocation: Are truck drivers—the same drivers who transport our food, clothing, building materials, and church sound systems—less significant *to God?*

---

[3] "Standard Occupational Classification," last modified March 11, 2010,
 http://www.bls.gov/soc/2010/soc530000.htm.

Ultimately, the only true measure of significance is how much something or someone is valued by God. But many people mistakenly believe that God only values ministry work, because it deals with eternal souls. In their minds, ministry is the only work that counts for eternity; it's the only work that is *eternally significant.* They assume God places little, if any, lasting value on work that deals with the temporal things of everyday life. The implied ranking of our vocations is obvious. Additionally, when someone who holds that belief isn't careful with his words, it sounds as if he is applying that same ranking to each person's individual value to God. Our superstar probably didn't mean to imply that truck drivers are less significant to God, but that's what many of us heard.

I've listened to hundreds of similar testimonies in seminars, conferences, and churches across the continent. You've probably heard them, too. Missionaries, pastors, and relief workers stand up and tell us about making the leap from nearly every profession imaginable. They answered the "higher call" to full-time ministry. They cast aside their marketplace jobs in order to do something more meaningful—something "for the Lord." Everyone else, the remaining workforce, looks up from a pew and listens to their stories—stories that are often laced with contempt for the speaker's former, "meaningless" work.

Audiences will sometimes affirm the speaker's decision to leap "from success to significance" by offering up an "Amen!" or "Hallelujah!" They may even give the speaker a stirring round of applause. But what's the truck driver—the one quietly sitting nine pews back, third from the left—feeling at that moment? And the accountant, engineer, retail associate, bank manager, and all the other people who will get up early the next morning and bend their backs at jobs just like the one the speaker renounced—what must they all feel at that moment?

They've told me. I've listened to their frustration, their unapplauded stories, and sometimes their despair. You see, I've been that speaker—the one standing on stage, receiving the applause. I'm a former corporate finance guy who became a missionary and then somehow wound up doing some public speaking, too. Whenever I speak, I like to hang around afterward and talk with individual audience members about their specific questions and concerns. As a result, I've had countless conversations with people who are looking for an answer to the question of significance. They sit in those pews and wonder, *Did I miss my calling in life? Is my life's work meaningless to God? Is ministry the only way to impact eternity?* Sometimes they lower their eyes in resignation and guilt—vocational guilt. But that guilt is a lie.

HOW WE UNINTENTIONALLY PERPETUATE THE LIE

It's crazy, but you and I, and millions of people just like us, have built a cultural paradigm that expects—even demands—that deeds of eternal value must fit neatly into the narrow box of religious service (or maybe into the slightly larger box of benevolent humanitarianism).

Have you been on a two-week, church-sponsored volunteer missions trip lately? Why did you go? Year after year, I've asked that question to battalions of eager volunteers who just landed on the mission field where I live. "You've traveled thousands of miles, sacrificed two weeks of vacation time, and spent a ton of money in order to work on a missions project. Why?" The answer is always the same: "To do some work for the Lord. To make a difference. To do something that counts for eternity." I listen to those words and then silently wonder, *What does that answer imply about the other fifty weeks of their year—the other 96 percent of their lives?* We've defined the box of eternal significance, and it's too small for 96 percent of a hardworking layperson's life.

If you hang around church people for more than about thirty seconds, you'll hear it. We use code phrases like "from success to significance" and "secular versus sacred." We have people in full-time ministry, part-time ministry, and extensive volunteer ministry; then there's everybody else. And there's little doubt about each person's ranking on the unspoken scale of eternal value.

Just listen to a group of elderly ladies comparing the careers of their grown children. They may be sipping tea and nibbling ginger snaps at a church ladies' luncheon, but underneath the pleasantries, there's a fierce game in play: it's the game of significance. Mrs. Hayes mentions that her son, an employee at the local car dealership, was just promoted to vice president of sales. Mrs. Williams artfully one-ups her with a comment about her daughter's responsibilities as the CEO of a large marketing firm. But then dear old Mrs. Evans, quiet until now, clears her throat and throws down the trump card. "My son and his family just moved to China to serve the Lord as missionaries." Silence . . . game over.

We regularly invite missionaries to stand up in front of our churches. Everyone *oohs* and *aahs* over their stories, and then we praise their work. But when was the last time your church invited a vice president of sales up to the podium and listened to the challenges he faces in his daily work? When was the last time everyone—or for that matter, *anyone*—listened to your story and praised your work?

In light of this reality, many Christians naturally conclude that marketplace vocations are less important to God than ministry vocations. I know; I've been there. When I was a corporate finance leader, I was never invited to speak in churches or at faith-based conferences. It seemed like religious leaders didn't care about what I did for a living. But then one day, I received a phone call that changed all of that.

NEW COURSE

We had a picture-perfect life. Then Phil called.

Misty and I seemed to have it all: great marriage; adorable kids; successful corporate career; charming old house on a tree-lined street in Greenville, South Carolina; and Henry's Southern-Style Barbecue Smokehouse only minutes away. Life could hardly get any better. That's when my phone rang.

Phil was a missionary to the remote villages of Alaska. A friend had given him my number. His proposition was straightforward—and radical: "Would you and Misty be willing to give up everything and move to Alaska to be missionaries? We need a missionary up here who has a background in business—someone to manage the increasingly complex administration of our growing missionary team."

"Um, Phil, do they serve southern-style barbecue in Alaska?"

Three weeks later, Misty and I were in a tiny airplane, fighting turbulence and high winds as we made our way through Alaska's narrow mountain passes. Our destination was a tiny village—and possibly our future home. We were checking it out to see if Phil's proposition and ministry were legitimate. Yep, Phil and his team were the real deal. They were trying to establish churches in the remote bush villages that dot the northern landscape. And they needed business administration help—big-time.

We sold our house, packed up the kids, and moved to rural Alaska—a place where *pest control* means keeping grizzly bears out of your garbage, winter temperatures drop to fifty degrees *below* zero, and no, they don't serve southern-style barbecue.

Today, when people ask me how Misty and I received "the call into the ministry," I tell them this simple story: I received a phone call from a missions organization, they had a specific need, we were in a position to help meet that need, we had a desire to meet that need, and wise friends and mentors encouraged us to go for it. That's it. Our call wasn't rocket science, and it certainly wasn't a mystical experience.

But something curious started to happen after we became missionaries. Pastors in the lower forty-eight states started asking me to come and speak to their congregations. I was a brand-new, clueless missionary. I still hadn't figured out what missionaries actually do all day long. But the pastors didn't care. They told me they wanted a missionary speaker "who connects with the congregation." Huh? I didn't understand. However, my first speaking engagement at a church missions conference made everything clear—painfully clear.

The conference organizers booked me as the final speaker in a lineup of six missionaries. *Six?* I was dumbfounded. *Will anyone*

show up on a Saturday to sit through six missionary presentations?
Unbelievably, people poured in—lots of them. *Oh, no! What have I
gotten myself into? Now I'm gonna have to stand up and say something to all these people.*

The other five speakers were *real* missionaries—veterans of the
craft. They looked like missionaries. They sounded like missionaries. And then there was me. I didn't fit. *What am I doing here? I'm
going to embarrass everybody and ruin the whole conference.*

The nightmare went something like this: the first missionary,
an older gentleman, stepped up to the microphone and spoke with
grave earnestness. "God called me to the mission field when I was
a senior in high school. . . ." All I could think was, *You've got to be
kidding me! An eighteen-year-old guy was seriously thinking about
missions? I had only one thing on my mind when I was eighteen—and
she was* not *the call to the mission field.* The missionary gentleman
then told us spellbinding stories about narrowly escaping death
behind the former Iron Curtain, starting a seminary in a country
few of us had ever heard of, and smuggling Bibles into hostile
lands.

The second missionary, a kindhearted lady, stood up and spoke
in hushed tones. "When I was ten years old, my grandmother read
me the story of the great pioneering missionary, Amy Carmichael.
While she was reading, I sensed God's leading in my life. He was
calling me into his service. From that day forward, I wanted to be
just like Amy. . . ." The third missionary was fifteen when he saw a
vision of Africa's lost souls falling into the fiery abyss. The fourth
missionary was only eight when he listened to a powerful sermon
about the world's lost and dying, and that's when God called him
into missions.

By this point, I half-expected the fifth missionary to say he'd been called just like John the Baptist. "My pregnant mother was listening to a guest missionary speaker at church, and I leapt in her womb." But he didn't say that. Instead, he said something about hearing a "still, small voice" at Bible college, placing his all on the altar, and serving God in the snake-infested jungles of South America.

There was one more speaker to go—me. The hike up to the platform was like climbing Everest. My heart was pounding. *Is this really happening? Are these other missionaries really humans? I shouldn't be here. There's been a horrible mistake. What am I going to say?* Finally, I stepped onto the podium and turned to face the audience.

What I saw changed my life. I looked out into a sea of desolate eyes—hard-working people who earned their daily bread in the everyday labors of the marketplace. Something was wrong—terribly wrong. They had come to the conference in eager hopes of discovering a link between their temporal lives and the eternal impact of world missions. But instead, their yearning hearts had just been bludgeoned by five hopelessly impossible examples of what it means to be called, of what it means to live a life that counts for eternity—of what it means to be significant to God.

With each consecutive speaker, the chasm between their everyday lives and a meaningful life in God's service grew wider and wider. They were worlds apart—an impossible leap. They felt hopeless. Their weary eyes said it all.

At that moment, I determined to one day show them the spectacular truth—the truth that their lives made a difference that would last forever, their vocations were significant, and they matter to God. But at that particular moment, the only words that came to mind were, "Uh, when I was eight years old, I didn't have a clue what the preacher was saying. I was daydreaming about fishin' and shootin' my BB gun. And, uh, when I was ten, I mostly wanted to be just like . . . um . . . Spider-Man."

The audience laughed; but more importantly, life flashed back into their eyes. The look on their faces—the look of hope—was the seed that grew into the book you are now reading.

AN IMPORTANT DISTINCTION

Early in this book, we need to establish an important distinction: freedom from vocational guilt is not freedom to live a life of selfish indulgence. This distinction is important, because many fear that vocational freedom is simply a license to live selfishly. But that fear is rooted in a deep misunderstanding—the assumption that marketplace work is inherently selfish.

Marketplace work is not inherently *selfish* work. And religious service is not inherently *selfless* work. Yes, we can choose to be idiots and work for selfish, prideful reasons. But that's true for religious employees as well as for scientists, stock market analysts, lumberjacks, pastry chefs, and everyone else who works in the marketplace. It's the attitude of our heart, not the classification of our job, that determines our motives. There's a ton of confusion surrounding this distinction, as illustrated by the following example.

"You have credibility," the pastor said to me over the phone. "You had what everyone is grasping for, and you gave it all up to serve God." That's the answer I received from a pastor when I asked him why he thought I would connect with his congregation. He continued, "We'd love for you to tell our people how you left the secular business world [which he had earlier described as a life of selfish ambition] and entered into the Lord's service."

I finally understood what he wanted me to say to his people and why he wanted me to connect. I was credible proof that the pursuit of success in the marketplace is vain and empty selfishness, that a person could give it all up and find fulfillment in a life sold-out for God in Christian ministry, and that even a businessperson can take the leap of faith and land on the promises of God.

What's not to like about any of that? It sounds like powerful truth that is anchored in the bedrock of the Bible—almost. Peel back the good intentions, and we find a subtle misunderstanding laced all throughout this sincere pastor's words. He's unaware of it, but there's an underlying assumption twisting the truth. It's been embedded into his thinking—yours and mine, too. Many of us trip over the deeply rooted assumption that working in a job that seemingly has nothing to do with God or faith is automatically less spiritual, less meaningful, and more self-centered than ministry work.

This is a serious dilemma for millions of Christians, because 95 percent of all Christians in the world earn their living in regular, everyday marketplace jobs.[4] Oh, sure, we've developed dozens of ways to get around the dilemma: earn money to give to the church, be a witness at work, squeeze in a few pro bono hours, and so on. But when we boil it all down, there's no getting around the fact that countless Christians assume that their work, at its core, is for self—that it's selfish. There's just one major problem with that assumption—it's a lie! It's a strand in the overall web of vocational guilt.

---

[4] Definitions and estimates vary. The London Institute for Contemporary Christianity estimates 98 percent. See Mark Greene, *The Great Divide* (London: LICC, 2010), 11.

We've built a guilt-ridden standard based on the external dividing line between marketplace work and ministry work. We're busy measuring externals, but all the while, God is looking directly at our hearts. "For the Lord sees not as man sees: man looks on the outward appearance, but the Lord looks on the heart."[5]

When we automatically equate marketplace work with selfishness, we confuse two entirely different, unrelated issues. It's like comparing chocolate-coated cherries to chocolate-coated crabapples. Last summer, Misty and I transplanted some crabapple trees to our property. They look great, but the crabapples are paralyzingly bitter. They're horrible to eat; not even the bears and moose, common visitors around our house, will eat them. Chocolate-coated crabapples and chocolate-coated cherries may look the same on the outside, but mix them together in your big sister's snack box, and you'll soon discover that there's an absolute, fundamental difference between them. Trust me.

Work is a gift from God. It is a major part of the role we play in God's masterpiece of eternity—and that includes marketplace work.

Selfishness is stupid. God hates it. It will destroy you.

Freedom from vocational guilt is not freedom to waste our lives bouncing from one shopping buzz or thrill-seeking high to the next. And it's not freedom to toss a few bags of rice at the feet of the world's hungry while we belly up to lifestyles of super-sized gluttony, all the while shrugging our consumption off as "enjoying the fruits of our labor." No, freedom from vocational guilt is none of that. All of that is like sucking on a chocolate-coated crabap-

---

5 1 Samuel 16:7

ple—it'll taste great for about two seconds, and then you'll experience devastating regret.

Freedom from vocational guilt is a good and glorious gift from God. It gives eyes to our deep ache for purpose and meaning. It frees our yearning hearts to see the Master at work, forging the breathtaking, the indescribable, the new heaven and earth united under the eternal reign of the Lord of glory—his masterpiece. Astonishingly, we'll see him forging it within the context of our regular, everyday lives.

God's great epic of eternity isn't just happening out there somewhere. It's taking place, in part, within the routine activities of laundry, sales meetings, production schedules, software installations, and Saturday afternoon chicken casseroles. When our eyes see the Master at work, the tasks that formerly seemed trivial and inconsequential (or even inherently selfish) will take on extraordinary significance and meaning. We'll lose ourselves in the wonder of it all—in the wonder of the Master.

CHAPTER 2

WHY WE BELIEVE THE LIE

If you need me, I'll be in my cubicle trying to imagine what futility doesn't feel like.

—*Dilbert*[1]

A slave is a living tool, just as a tool is an inanimate slave.

—Aristotle[2]

Thus says the Lord God: Because you make your heart like the heart of a god, therefore, behold . . . you shall die the death of the slain.

—Ezekiel 28:6–8

---

[1] Scott Adams, *14 Years of Loyal Service in a Fabric-Covered Box: A Dilbert Book* (Kansas City: Andrews McMeel, 2009), 10.

[2] Aristotle, Politics 1.1255, quoted in Darrow L. Miller with Marit Newton, *LifeWork: A Biblical Theology for What You Do Every Day* (Seattle: YWAM, 2009), 277.

W e're prone to believe the lie of vocational guilt for three major reasons: our history, the sense of futility that overshadows much of our work, and our pride. In this chapter, we'll explore each of these.

The constant presence of these factors in our lives makes believing the lie as easy as breathing. We simply believe it without thinking about it, and then we applaud the truck driver who quit trucking in order to become an assistant pastor.

WE'VE HEARD IT A VERY LONG TIME

It all started roughly 2,300 years ago when the Greek philosophers Plato and Aristotle sought to distinguish their lives from the brute, animal-like futility of physical working life. To these philosophers, work was a curse—nothing more. They saw work as slavish bondage to the physical demands of our temporal bodies: we work to eat, eat to survive, reproduce somewhere along the way, die like animals, disintegrate into oblivion, and then vanish from the memory of the world. In the end, it's all pointless futility, identical to the life of a beast.

A human, however, is endowed with a single, distinguishing capacity—a gift that sets him or her apart from the animals and lifts him or her above raw futility. Humans have the capacity for knowledge—the ability to think, reason, and contemplate. Hence, according to the ancient Greek philosophers, contemplation of higher things is the only truly human activity. Therefore, an authentic human life is a life spent in contemplation, not earthly toil. Furthermore, "to the degree and at the time we engage in contemplative thought, we become like the gods."[3]

But on the flip side, these philosophers viewed a life spent working to meet the demands of bodily existence in the physical world—*the secular world*—as not being a human life at all; it was merely the temporal life of an animal in human form. Thus the Greeks developed a dichotomy in which the lower physical realm was futile and essentially evil while the higher realm—*the spiritual realm*—of contemplation had eternal value and was good.[4] Today we refer to this two-tier philosophy as *Greek dualism* or *Platonic dualism.*

But these Greek philosophers had a dilemma on their hands. Someone had to grow the grain, build the houses, cook the meals, and repair the cobblestone streets. Someone had to be . . . *less than human.* They overcame this dilemma with a simple, age-old solution—slavery. Aristotle stated it bluntly when he wrote, "A slave is a living tool, just as a tool is an inanimate slave."[5] In this system, a wealthy Greek could relegate the futile work of the physical realm to his slaves and thus spend his days focusing on the non-physical realm—the things that have eternal value. What a great system—unless you're a slave. And many of the early New Testament church believers were slaves. They were slaves who did

[3] Lee Hardy, *The Fabric of This World: Inquiries Into Calling, Career Choice, and the Design of Human Work* (Grand Rapids, MI: William B. Eerdmans, 1990), 12.
[4] For a more detailed summary of Greek thought on work, see Lee Hardy, *The Fabric of This World*, 6–16.
[5] Aristotle, Politics 1.1255, quoted in Darrow L. Miller, *LifeWork*, 277.

the work most of us would now define as *marketplace* work or *secular* work.

When the apostles carried Christianity into the Gentile world, they carried it into a culture saturated with Greek philosophy. Almost immediately, that philosophy began seeping into the church. The apostles Paul and John battled it head-on in their defenses of the incarnation and resurrection of Jesus Christ. "It's no coincidence," writes Randy Alcorn, "that Paul wrote his detailed defense of physical resurrection to the Corinthians, who were immersed in the Greek philosophy of dualism. They'd been taught that the spiritual was incompatible with the physical."[6] To someone immersed in Greek dualism, Jesus' physical resurrection would be unthinkable, because only the *spirit* is everlasting. As we'll see in part two of this book, the Bible strongly refutes this view. Yet from the time of the apostle Paul until now, ancient Greek philosophy has infiltrated and profoundly influenced the Christian church.

Church fathers such as Eusebius, Augustine, Thomas Aquinas, and many others split the Christian life into upper and lower spheres. They relegated marketplace work to the lower, futile realm, and they elevated the work of Christian ministry to the upper, eternal realm. Reflecting on this deeply rooted error, Os Guinness writes, "Higher vs. lower, sacred vs. secular, perfect vs. permitted, contemplation vs. action . . . the dualism and elitism in this view need no underscoring. Sadly this 'two-tier' or 'double-life' view of calling flagrantly perverted biblical teaching by nar-

---

6 Randy Alcorn, *Heaven* (Carol Stream, IL: Tyndale House, 2004), 475.

rowing the sphere of calling and excluding most Christians from its scope. It also dominated later Christian thinking."[7]

Today the church is permeated by this two-tier, dualistic value system, which causes us to think that assistant pastors are obviously more valuable to God than truck drivers. Even within the ministry profession, there's an understood ranking of significance. Missionaries who work among unreached people groups are often at the top of the list, because their work seemingly has the greatest impact on eternal souls. Further down are teaching pastors. Lower still are administrative pastors . . . and on down it goes. The entire ranking system is a lie, but we've heard it for a very, very long time.

The Dualistic Sacred-Secular Divide

If it were true that the "sacred" work of Christian ministry is the only work that counts for eternity, then most of us would be destined to spend our lives in vocations that have no eternal value—the entire nonprofit sector, which includes nearly all faith-based ministries, employs only 6 percent of the US workforce.[8]

Consequently, if we wanted to do something that is significant in God's eyes, most of us would have to find ministry opportunities outside the context of our paid employment. But at best, the average adult with kids to feed and bills to pay can dedicate roughly 5 percent of his or her time to the activities we tradition-

---

ally define as ministry. That's about 8.5 hours per week. A few committed volunteers may be able to squeeze in a whopping 17 hours each week, but even then, we're only talking about 10 percent of their time. In truth, full-time ministry employees aren't much better off; their 45 hour ministry jobs account for only 27 percent of the total hours in a week.

So what does God think of the other 95 or 90 or 73 percent of our time—of our lives? Is it merely secular? Is it tolerated but not valued by God? Throughout the remainder of this book, we will explore the Bible's answer to that question. For now, let's see what happens when we blindly accept the widely held, dualistic assumption that those hours (and the activities we do during those hours) have no eternal value.

When we make that assumption, we quickly find ourselves living two separate lives. We live a sliver of life that makes a difference in eternity, but everything else we do, the great bulk of life, has no eternal value—or worse, it's a necessary evil. (Somebody has to do it.) We want to do work that matters to God, but the everyday demands of life constantly pull us in the opposite direction. The tension is relentless. That tension is vocational guilt.

"One of the greatest hindrances to internal peace which the Christian encounters," writes A. W. Tozer, "is the common habit of dividing our lives into two areas, the sacred and the secular."[9] The "sacred-secular heresy,"[10] as Tozer calls it, splits our lives and causes an overwhelming amount of confusion among Christians today. From time to time, we inevitably glance at our sliver of significance on the sacred side of the divide. Then we look over at our great heap of meaninglessness on the secular side. Regret grips us,

---

[9] A. W. Tozer, *The Pursuit of God* (Camp Hill, PA: Christian Publications, 1993), 109.
[10] Tozer, *The Pursuit of God,* 117.

and then we plummet into confusion, frustration, and guilt. Referring to this tension, Tozer writes:

> Most Christians are caught in its trap. They cannot get a satisfactory adjustment between the claims of the two worlds. They try to walk the tightrope between two kingdoms and they find no peace in either. Their strength is reduced, their outlook confused and their joy taken from them. I believe this state of affairs is wholly unnecessary. We have gotten ourselves on the horns of a dilemma, true enough, but the dilemma is not real. It is a creature of misunderstanding. The sacred-secular antithesis has no foundation in the New Testament.[11]

The sacred-secular divide is a deadly lie. It has no place in the Christian faith. Mark Greene, Executive Director of The London Institute for Contemporary Christianity, argues that the sacred-secular divide is "the biggest challenge facing the church today."[12] Greene later states that because of the divide, "the message of the gospel is being partially eclipsed and that this has led to a narrower, less radical, less adventurous understanding of what it means to follow Jesus than the Bible's compelling picture."[13]

As we become accustomed to living in two separate worlds, the church gradually loses all relevance to our weekday lives. Church is church; work is work. We navigate between two unrelated spheres, two value systems, two moral codes. We begin to

---

[11] Tozer, *The Pursuit of God*, 111.
[12] Greene, *The Great Divide*, 1.
[13] Greene, *The Great Divide*, 5.

confine our faith to the sacred side of the divide—that sliver of time we spend doing "religious stuff." The rest of the time—the great bulk of the time—our faith is off duty. It sits on the sidelines, unconsidered and unexpressed. Edward A. White speaks with forthright clarity when he writes:

> We live in a culture that measures our worth by our accomplishments (justification by works). This is in direct conflict with the Gospel of justification by grace. We can handle the dichotomy if we can separate church from the rest of life. As long as the two are separated, we will not experience conflict. Six days a week we can be driven by the compulsive need to climb the ladder of success. On the seventh day we can smile, shake hands, and sing hymns about "Amazing Grace."[14]

When we divide our lives in this way, our walk with God gradually recedes to nothing more than an obscure fragment of life. We no longer *live* a life of faith. Instead, we (occasionally) *go* and *do* acts of faith, perhaps squeezing in as much as seventeen exhausting hours each week—and maybe even a two-week missions trip. But deep in our hearts, we know something is dangerously wrong; in severing the sacred from the secular, we've ripped eternity out of the context of our vocations. We've ripped our faith out of our everyday life.

---

[14] White, quoted in Robert J. Banks, *Faith Goes to Work: Reflections from the Marketplace* (Eugene, OR: Wipf and Stock, 1999), 7.

FUTILITY

Research shows that Monday morning is by far the most common time for heart attacks.[15] Is anyone surprised by this? A sense of dread overwhelms countless people as they wake up to face yet another workweek. In some instances, it stops their hearts. Let's face it—work is grueling, and little, if any, of our daily toil feels even remotely significant in the grand scheme of eternity. Pulitzer Prize-winning author Studs Terkel didn't pull any punches in the opening lines of his literary portrait of everyday work, a book he titled, simply, *Working:*

> This book, being about work, is, by its very nature, about violence—to the spirit as well as to the body. It is about ulcers as well as accidents, about shouting matches as well as fistfights, about nervous breakdowns as well as kicking the dog around. It is, above all (or beneath all), about daily humiliations. To survive the day is triumph enough for the walking wounded among the great many of us.[16]

Many people reflect on the frustrating reality of their work and sigh, *Dear Lord, is this really it? Is this seriously what you want me to do with my life? And what does it matter, anyway? I'm just going to leave it all behind someday.* The author of Ecclesiastes appears

[15] "Monday Morning Heart Attacks . . . and Other Health Risks by the Day of the Week," last updated February 24, 2011, http://health.msn.com/health-topics/monday-morning-heart-attacks-and-other-health-risks-by-the-day-of-the-week.

[16] Studs Terkel, *Working: People Talk about What They Do All Day and How They Feel about What They Do* (New York: New Press, 1997), xi.

to have been thinking the same thing when he wrote, "I hated all my toil in which I toil under the sun, seeing that I must leave it to the man who will come after me."[17]

We humans, stripped of all delusions, stagger under the soul-crushing weight of futility. Like a prizefighter, full of confidence, we step into the ring of working life. Thousands of hours of education and training have honed us into finely tuned working machines. But somewhere in the fight, often in the midlife rounds, we're stunned by the uppercut of futility—*this is all temporal; it makes no lasting difference.* Some look for meaning elsewhere. Some slug it out, dead on their feet. Others buckle.

Few examples portray the horror of meaningless labor more vividly than the story of Eugene Heimler, a Hungarian Jew who survived the German concentration camp Tröglitz. He and his fellow prisoners were repeatedly forced to haul sand from one end of the prison work area to the other, then turn around and haul it all back to its original place. Heimler wrote:

> Day after day, week after week, we had to carry the sand to and fro, until gradually people's minds began to give way. . . . In the face of a completely meaningless task people started to lose their sanity. Some went berserk and tried to run away, only to be shot by the guards; others ran against the electrified wire fence and burnt themselves to death. . . . The suicide rate in Tröglitz went up as a result of this. . . . It was clear that meaningless tasks and pointless work destroyed people.[18]

---

[17] Ecclesiastes 2:18
[18] Eugene Heimler, *Mental Illness and Social Work* (Harmondsworth, Middlesex, England: Penguin Books, 1967), 107–108.

Deep down, many of us believe we labor in meaningless tasks and pointless work. We feel like we're moving sand from one end of the prison to the other. Pull a weed today; two weeds crop up tomorrow. Give up your weekend to write a report for your boss; he doesn't even read it. Spend two years designing and installing ergonomically improved workstations in a factory; a foreign owner shuts down the factory and lays off all the employees, including you. Write a computer program today; someone changes the operating system tomorrow. Earlier today, I glanced out my office window and saw that the tire on my utility trailer, the tire I patched last week, is flat—again. On and on it goes.

I hate to be a killjoy here, but it appears that we'll spend an entire lifetime frantically working on stuff that wears out, falls apart, and eventually winds up in a landfill—*and then we'll die.* Sooner or later, our life's work will completely vanish from the face of the earth—almost as if we never even existed. Late in his life, Mark Twain grappled with the fate of humankind, and cynical despair flowed from his pen:

> A myriad of men are born; they labor and sweat and struggle for bread. . . . Age creeps upon them; infirmities follow. . . . They vanish from a world where they were of no consequence; where they achieved nothing; where they were a mistake and a failure and a foolishness; where they have left no sign they have existed—a world which will lament them a day and forget them forever.[19]

---

[19] Mark Twain, *The Autobiography of Mark Twain* (New York: HarperCollins, 2000), 250.

Faced with this dismal prospect, many of us embark on a quest to do something significant—something that will last for all eternity—before it's too late. We think, *Surely this isn't what God wants me to be doing. He's just got to have something more meaningful for me than this—something that makes a difference.* Then along comes a well-intended friend or seminar speaker who says, "If you want to beat the futility blues and accomplish something that will last forever, then you need to start looking at your ministry options—the options that will airlift you to the highest peaks of meaning and purpose." However, if we listen closely to their message, we won't hear the truth of the Bible. Instead, we'll hear the undertones of a deeply rooted lie—one that we've heard for a very, very long time.

A False Solution to Futility

Significance sells. This fact makes perfect sense in light of the apparent futility of our lives. But we are selling a lie when we use eternal significance as a ministry recruiting tool. There are organizations that seek to recruit people out of the marketplace workforce by trolling the bait of significance through the waters of vocational guilt. "Hey, your life has been a meaningless exercise in the pursuit of success, which we all know is pointless futility. So join our team, and do something meaningful for God with the rest of your life." Their intentions are good, but their primary recruiting tool is a glittering, treble-hooked deception: they imply that we can grasp significance by shifting over to the sacred side of the divide.

"They go wrong in thinking that 'success' failed to satisfy because it was secular whereas 'significance' will be fulfilling because it is religious,"[20] writes Os Guinness. The foundation of our value to God and our personal fulfillment runs far deeper than all such shallow formulations of significance, meaning, and purpose. As sons and daughters of God, our eternal worth is not based on what we do. It is based, rather, on whose we are. Apart from this truth, writes Guinness, "all hope of discovering purpose (as in the current talk of shifting 'from success to significance') will end in disappointment."[21]

We can gain some perspective on this popular recruiting tool by asking a simple question: What would happen if every single professing Christian on the planet (roughly one-third of the global workforce) said, "Okay, I'm in; sign me up"? In other words, what would happen if, next Monday morning, we all quit our marketplace jobs and charged out to do something more significant in full-time Christian ministry? Basically, the world would shut down. Major infrastructures and economies would collapse, and soon entire segments of the world population would lack food and other basic necessities. "Man shall not live by bread alone"[22] —but he will starve to death without it.

God, in his sovereignty, apparently created a system where most of us *must* work in the secular world—otherwise the human race would go extinct. It's like a sick game of musical chairs; there aren't enough significant seats to go around. When the music stops, the vast majority of us will still be standing. We'll still be insignificant; our labor will have no eternal value. We're trapped.

---

[20] Guinness, *The Call*, 143.
[21] Guinness, *The Call*, 4.
[22] Matthew 4:4

We're trapped between the demands of survival and our twisted theologies of vocation and calling.

If we make the leap into ministry or humanitarian relief work because we believe that jobs like painting houses, preparing tax returns, and managing industrial warehouses have no eternal value, then who do we expect to do those jobs for us? Someone less significant? Someone who must toil his or her life away in futility because we have more meaningful things to do? The dualism underlying this belief is self-evident, and it should have no place whatsoever in our ministry-recruiting playbooks.

Da Vinci and Daniel: Two Responses to Futility

Perhaps it's best to drive this discussion home with a contrast between two historic lives: da Vinci of Renaissance Italy and Daniel of the Old Testament. These two men had brilliant minds but radically different responses to the apparent futility of their life's work. Leonardo da Vinci died in despair; Daniel saw sparks fly on the white-hot ingot of God's eternal masterpiece.

The cause of da Vinci's anguish was the devastating realization that his days were fleeting and futile. He hoped to accomplish much more; he dreamed of attaining perfection in his work, but it was too late. As he neared death, most of his works were unfinished; some had already been destroyed. His hopes and dreams were an impossibility. In the last months of his life, he saw the true horror of it all. He traveled to Milan to see his great work, *The Last Supper,* and there he found it already disintegrating. The few masterpieces he finished were crumbling before his eyes. Shortly before he died, he wrote these dismal words: "We should not desire the impossible."[23]

Da Vinci, one of the most gifted minds in human history, went to his grave believing the lie. The question haunted him to the very end: *Did any of it really matter?* Da Vinci ran against the electrified wire fence of futility, and on those crackling wires, all his hope died.

Daniel, in stark contrast, saw God's epic of eternity play out before his own eyes. He didn't pine away, wallowing in the futility blues—but he had every right to. We need to clear away a heap of confusion. Most of us have a goofy conception of Daniel's life. We assume his days were a continuous saga of hanging out in the lion's den, interpreting King Nebuchadnezzar's dreams, experiencing mind-blowing prophetic visions, and seeing bizarre handwriting on the wall—all of it extraordinary stuff. He did do all of that. But all of that amazing prophet stuff made up only a small part of his life—maybe a grand total of 10 percent. What about the other 90 percent of his life? What did he actually do all day long, day after day, year after year?

Apart from a few spectacular exceptions, Daniel—much like the rest of us—slogged through a routine daily grind. He was an extremely talented guy with a detestable job. He was a slave; his owner was the pagan king of Babylon. He spent his days toiling away in a mind-numbing government bureaucracy. His coworkers were backstabbers. His department was infested with pagan sorcery and idolatry, and the corporate cafeteria served up a cuisine that defiled his conscience. He spent his entire adult life working for the nation that sacked his home town, Jerusalem, and his first

---

[23] Leonardo da Vinci, *Thoughts on Art and Life,* trans. Maurice Baring (Boston: Merrymount Press, 1906), 55.

day on the job may have involved a little outpatient procedure involving a knife and a pair of pliers. Castration—what a great way to kick off your new career.[24]

It would be hard to beat the crushing futility of Daniel's job. He spent his entire life building up Babylon, about which God said, "The broad wall of Babylon shall be leveled to the ground, and her high gates shall be burned with fire. The peoples labor for nothing, and the nations weary themselves only for fire."[25] Daniel spent a lifetime toiling away on a project that God specifically said was "for nothing . . . only for fire."

The part that truly flies in the face of our distorted notion of significance is this: even though Babylon was in the center of God's obliterating crosshairs, God told Daniel and all the other exiles to work hard, build Babylon up, support it, and make it prosper:

> Thus says the Lord of hosts, the God of Israel, to all the exiles whom I have sent into exile from Jerusalem to Babylon: Build houses and live in them; plant gardens and eat their produce. . . . Multiply there, and do not decrease. But seek the welfare of the city where I have sent you into exile, and pray to the Lord on its behalf, for in its welfare you will find your welfare. (Jeremiah 29:4–7)

So what did Daniel do? Did he grumble, sulk, write something dismal like, "We should not desire the impossible," and then die in despair? Not a chance. Instead, he lived his life all-in. He

---

[24] First Century historian Josephus stated that Daniel was made to be a eunuch. See Josephus, *The Antiquities of the Jews*, X.10.1.
[25] Jeremiah 51:58

flourished fearlessly, clear to the very end. He was a man brimming with confidence—not in himself, but in God. Daniel knew that he was part of something spectacular, something that transcended time. Where others saw crushing futility, Daniel saw an everlasting masterpiece.

As crazy as it must have seemed, Daniel threw his extraordinary talent into the futile abyss of Babylon. He never doubted; he knew he was standing in his own allotted place in the epic of eternity, *because God put him there.* Like master to apprentice, God entrusted the hammer to Daniel's hand. He said, "Strike it. Strike it right here. This is your place. This is where I want you to shape eternity."

The overarching theme of the book of Daniel is simple but also unsearchable. It is the bedrock of all that exists and the secret to Daniel's life. The theme of Daniel is God's absolute sovereignty, "that the living may know that the Most High rules the kingdom of men."[26] Daniel had unwavering trust in the hand of the Master. So he lived his life—his seemingly futile, toilsome life. The hammer fell. Sparks flew, and the Master was delighted.

Daniel's book concludes with God's ringing words: "Go your way till the end. And you shall rest and shall stand in your allotted place at the end of the days."[27] Nearly three thousand years later, those words ring in our ears, too. In them, we discover the ultimate meaning and eternal significance of our daily toil. The significance of it all is wrapped up in the glory of the one who gives us our place in the epic. When we see his sovereign hand in our lives, then nothing is ever small, mundane, or futile. Instead, we hear the echo of the Master's hammer, and we see sparks fly.

---

[26] Daniel 4:17
[27] Daniel 12:13

PRIDE

"A shrill cry rang out in the night; and he felt a pain like a dart of poisoned ice pierce his left shoulder."[28]

Frodo survived the wound. But the poison of the Morgul-knife sought Frodo's heart for the rest of his days in Middle Earth. Not until he sailed away to Valinor, the Undying Lands, did he find complete healing from that poisonous blade.

The Black Riders sought to pierce Frodo's heart. "If they had succeeded," Gandalf the Grey explained, "you would have become like they are, only weaker and under their command. You would have become a wraith under the domain of the Dark Lord."[29]

J. R. R. Tolkien's *Lord of the Rings* paints the picture vividly. Pride, like the poison of the Morgul-knife, seeks your heart—and mine, too. We'll not be free of it until we cross the river into eternity. On that victorious day, we will at last be free of our festering pride. Until then, however, we have a battle to fight.

In leering disdain, our pride sneers, *I will authenticate my own significance. I will prove my worth to God, to humankind, and to the universe. Glory to me in the highest.* And what better way to authenticate my own worth than to design a formula for significance that depends entirely on me? This is precisely what we've done.

In creating a false link between eternal value and a narrow list of sacred activities, we've made our significance depend on us. We've built a system that places our importance to God within the reach of our own, self-determining grasp. I can willfully choose to be valuable to God by entering into the ministry, going on a mis-

---

28 J. R. R. Tolkien, *The Lord of the Rings* (New York: Houghton Mifflin, 1994), 191.
29 Tolkien, *Lord of the Rings,* 216.

sions trip, volunteering more time at church, witnessing, praying, and studying the Bible. All of these activities center on my own choice and action. This formula for significance is a lie that makes much of me and little of God.

With this lie, we twist our formerly pure labors into vile acts of pride. The labors themselves are not bad or prideful. They're part of the God-ordained fabric of life—gifts and roles assigned by the Creator to various members of the body of Christ. Some of us need to be pastors; some of us, missionaries; many of us, volunteers; and all of us need to witness, pray, and study the Bible. Likewise, some of us need to be payroll administrators; some of us, air traffic controllers; some of us, receptionists; and 3.2 million of us need to be truck drivers. But here's the catch—none of those activities, whether ministry work or marketplace work, earn us favor with God or make us more significant in his eyes.

The world around us measures our worth by our accomplishments, but this value system stands in direct opposition to the gospel of grace. We cannot earn or prove our everlasting value to God. He alone bestows on each of us our worth. Jesus Christ's life, death, and resurrection purchased our everlasting lives. We are adopted as beloved sons and daughters of God. This adoption is a gift; we can do nothing but receive it and then worship him in awe. Our significance rests in the nail-scarred hands of Jesus Christ, not in choosing to participate in a narrow list of activities on the sacred side of an artificial divide that is "a creature of misunderstanding."[30]

---

[30] Tozer, *The Pursuit of God*, 111.

The Battle Ignited by Pride

Long ago, there was another being who desired significance. In a hideous instant, however, his desire turned to cosmic horror. The "son of dawn"—"the signet of perfection, full of wisdom and perfect in beauty"[31] —spurned the Lord God of heaven and earth. He sought to grasp significance by the power of his own might, and in so doing, he waged war to usurp the very throne of God. But God is God. Satan is not God. Satan grasped for the thing that only God can give, and in reaching, he fell.

> How you are fallen from heaven,
> O Day Star, son of Dawn!
> How you are cut down to the ground,
> you who laid the nations low!
> You said in your heart,
> "I will ascend to heaven;
> above the stars of God
> I will set my throne on high;
> I will sit on the mount of assembly
> in the far reaches of the north;
> I will ascend above the heights of the clouds;
> I will make myself like the Most High."
> But you are brought down to Sheol,
> to the far reaches of the pit. (Isaiah 14:12–15)

The devil is fallen; his destiny is Sheol. But today, before the return of Jesus Christ, you and I have a battle to fight. The epic battle of eternity is raging, and we're smack in the middle of it.

---

[31] Isaiah 14:12; Ezekiel 28:12

The sovereign Lord God Almighty could whisper a single word and end it all. The battle would be finished, Satan would be vanquished, and peace would reign forevermore. But instead, God ordained that his glory is most magnified by creating a masterpiece that is forged, in part, by the fire of cosmic war. He granted Satan a window of space and time to roam, and he assigned you and me lives to live right in the middle of it. This is our place; this is where the Master wants us to stand and fight. This is where we shape eternity.

CHAPTER 3

THE SUNDAY-MONDAY DISCONNECT

Clergy mistrusted pragmatism. It played into their caricature of the shallowness and hard-heartedness of businesspeople. Meanwhile the business community hooted over the clergy's "fuzzy-mindedness."

—Nash and McLennan[1]

I wish pastors had a clue. I want to be equipped on Sunday for what I face on Monday.

—Colman M. Mockler, former chairman of Gillette[2]

Now there are varieties of gifts, but the same Spirit; and there are varieties of service, but the same Lord; and there are varieties of activities, but it is the same God who empowers them all in everyone.

—1 Corinthians 12:4–6

---

[1] Laura Nash and Scotty McLennan, *Church on Sunday, Work on Monday: The Challenge of Fusing Christian Values with Business Life* (San Francisco: Jossey-Bass, 2001), 140.

[2] Colman M. Mockler, quoted in David W. Miller, *God at Work: The History and Promise of the Faith at Work Movement* (New York: Oxford University Press, 2007), 103.

If one of my kids staggers into our bedroom in the middle of the night, whimpers to Misty, "Mommy, my tummy hurts . . ." and then proceeds to spew the remnants of his or her supper onto the bedroom floor, I'm outta there. Gone! I can't take it. If I don't get fresh air fast, I'll join the volley. Before the kid even finishes the word *mommy*, I'm already sprinting out the back door of the house in my boxer shorts, gasping for air. There may be three feet of snow on the ground, and it may be forty degrees below zero outside, but I don't care. I need fresh air!

A couple of years ago, Misty flew to Colorado for a seven-day ladies' retreat. She knows I'm incompetent when left alone with our five children for an entire week, so before she left, she carefully prepared meals, organized clothing, wrote down schedules, and then handed me a detailed set of instructions on how to multitask. She made it all sound easy. Everything was going to be great— quality time with Daddy. All I had to do was remember each kid's name and follow Misty's instructions.

Just as she was pulling out of the driveway, waving good-bye for an entire week, *it* happened. Kid number four puked, big-time. He hit the couch, the table, the lamp—and his big sister's hair. If for nothing else, we had to award him a score of 9.8 for sheer presentation.

By 7:00 the next morning, three out of five kids were sick. Within forty-eight hours, four out of five were hurling their guts out. The experience scarred me for life.

We hardly touched the meals, the clothing was all trashed within two days, schedules were a total fiasco, and multitasking consisted of holding kids under the shower while at the same time spraying citrus-scented Lysol disinfectant directly up my own nostrils. Quality time with Daddy turned into the week of upchuck purgatory.

Life is like that. We sit in church on Sunday and listen to a carefully prepared sermon. It all makes perfect sense. It all seems clear. There's nothing to it; everything is going to be great. Then Monday comes. And life hurls on us.

Suddenly, there's a total disconnect between Sunday's sermon and the reality of Monday. Our weekday lives don't look anything like the pastor's sermon—not even close. In particular, the disconnect seems to be insurmountably wide whenever the pastor talks about our jobs in "the secular marketplace" or "the business world." In light of Monday's messiness, his sermonized advice and sweeping generalizations seem completely irrelevant to what we actually face in the workplace. As a result, many people fail to see any connection between their Sunday faith and their weekday work life.

Similarly, I could say Misty's carefully prepared schedules and instructions all seemed completely irrelevant. In light of my week of upchuck purgatory, they seemed idealistic and altogether unhelpful. There was a total disconnect. But I never got angry at Misty because of the disconnect, and I certainly didn't file for divorce when she returned home. It would be absurd to get angry at Misty and leave her because of the disconnect. Likewise, it would be absurd to get angry at our pastors and leave the church because of the Sunday-Monday disconnect.

My analogy isn't quite perfect. It breaks down, because there was nothing Misty could have done to preempt the quality-time-with-Daddy disconnect. Few pastors can say the same about the Sunday-Monday disconnect. However, blaming the entire problem on our pastors is still not the answer; it does nothing to bridge the disconnect. In this book, I level several points of criticism at the church. But we need to remember an important fact. Our pastors are not the church; *we are the church*. It's not all the pastor's fault; we also bear responsibility for the disconnect.

For instance, have we ever bothered to say to our pastors, "I appreciate your teaching, but in all honesty, I'm having a hard time connecting it to the reality of my workweek. How can we work together to bridge the disconnect?" A simple conversation that opens with those lines would be a giant first step in the right direction. Yet in our churches today, that conversation is extremely rare.[3] Consequently, the disconnect remains in place. It's a destructive feature of the church's established paradigm.

THE DISCONNECT CAUSES FRUSTRATION, CYNICISM, AND GUILT

William Diehl, a former sales manager with Bethlehem Steel, accurately viewed his sales work as an essential part of his God-given vocation and ministry to others. But when reflecting on his life-long experience in the church, he writes, "I have never been in a congregation where there was any type of public affirmation of a

---

[3] David W. Miller, *God at Work,* 83.

ministry in my career. In short, I must conclude that my church really doesn't have the least interest in whether or how I minister in my daily work." Diehl goes on to say, "There were times when I was made to feel guilty because a commitment to community . . . interfered with a request for service within the congregation. I am not alone in my disillusionment. . . . Many other laypeople too feel that the church has all but abandoned them in their weekday world."[4]

Diehl wrote those words back in 1976. Today, survey after survey confirms that Diehl's words "still ring true for a majority of churchgoers in the United States."[5] David Miller, Director of the Princeton University Faith & Work Initiative, summarizes a mountain of data when he writes, "We might think the church would be interested in being present in the whole of life, including the workplace where most parishioners spend the majority of their waking hours. . . . Yet, in these matters, the anecdotal and empirical evidence suggest just the opposite."[6]

Worse than being merely uninterested in the workweek lives of their members, "the pulpit all too frequently sends the signal that work in the church matters but work in the world does not."[7] Miller poignantly concludes, "The result is two classes of citizenship in Christian life, where many laypeople feel relegated to second-class status in the kingdom of God."[8]

Churchgoers are frustrated. Many feel their pastor devalues or even belittles their jobs—the same jobs that fill the offering plate, pay the pastor's salary, and support missionary endeavors through-

---

[4] William E. Diehl, *Christianity and Real Life* (Philadelphia: Fortress, 1976), vi–vii.
[5] David W. Miller, *God at Work*, 79–94.
[6] David W. Miller, *God at Work*, 79.
[7] David W. Miller, *God at Work*, 10.
[8] David W. Miller, *God at Work*, 92.

out the world. For some, the frustration eventually festers into raw cynicism; they begin to seethe with contempt for the pastor and the church. Researchers Laura Nash and Scotty McLennan conducted an extensive study on the relationship between the church and the workplace. In unvarnished terms, they concluded, "The businessperson sees little point. Why join a game [the church] in which you are the predetermined loser?"[9]

Pastors perceive themselves as being supportive and helpfully engaged in the work-life concerns of their flock. But many church members perceive just the opposite. There's clearly a disconnect between what the pastor thinks he says and what the rest of us think we hear. Making an effort to understand the factors driving that disconnect, as we will do in the remainder of this chapter, will go a long way toward helping us connect our Sunday faith to the complex reality of our weekday life.

THE VIEW FROM HERE

"My pastor doesn't have a clue what it's like at my workplace." Whenever I hear those words from a frustrated church member, I think to myself, *Well, of course he doesn't. How could he possibly have a clue what it's really like? He doesn't work in your job; you do. Cut the guy some slack.*

Church members should stop demanding that their pastors be all things to all people, and pastors should stop pretending to be all things to all people. We burn pastors out under the strain of such an impossible expectation. Besides, God didn't design the

---

[9] Nash and McLennan, *Church on Sunday, Work on Monday,* 243.

church to operate that way. He didn't bestow an all-encompassing skill set on any one of us.

We have different perspectives on work. For example, most of us went to a school—an engineering school, business school, tech school, or other type of school—geared toward equipping us for economic productivity. Pastors went to seminary; economic productivity wasn't even an elective. Now we all hang out together on Sundays and wonder why there's such a big disconnect. Pastors and church members are spring-loaded with vastly different perspectives on work. In the next few pages, we will look into just a handful of them—a sampler of sorts. My hope is that both pastors and church members alike will catch a glimpse of the view from the other side of the pulpit.

Sermon Depictions of the Marketplace

Let's start with an observation that we've already mentioned. There are exceptions, but the message we hear from the pulpit is often dismissive of marketplace work. We hear it in subtle ways. I recently listened to a sermon by one of the most popular preachers in the United States—a guy I highly respect and who would never intentionally disparage common, everyday labor. But while giving an illustration, he mentioned that he had to spend two hours cleaning his garage. Then he said, "I hate that. I'm gonna be spending two hours doing something that has no eternal value. . . . I want to do something eternal. I don't want to just sweep and clean and move boxes." While he was cleaning, his neighbor came over to pray with him, so everything turned out great in his illustration. But I couldn't help wondering how many millions of

Christians throughout the world earn their living by sweeping, cleaning, and moving boxes—not for two hours, but for a lifetime?

Again, there are many exceptions, but from the pulpit, some pastors depict the marketplace as little more than a venture in greed. Their body language, tone of voice, and words tend to simmer with low-grade antipathy for business and the marketplace—*the false god of mammon*. Obviously, we should all hate the false god of mammon; the problem is that these pastors view the entire business world through the lens of mammon. As David Miller notes, "this sweeping portrait of people in the marketplace does a gross injustice to the average person's workplace experience."[10] But if we step back and think about it from the pastors' point of view, *who can blame them?*

When a pastor is forced to slash the church missions budget on Thursday, then on Sunday look out across a sea of people who give on average less than 3 percent of their income,[11] it's hard to blame him for equating marketplace work with greed. We deserve it. If we don't give away our money lavishly, then we have no right to whine about our pastor's negative view of our work. The words of Matthew 7:3 come to mind: "Why do you see the speck that is in your brother's eye, but do not notice the log that is in your own eye?" Yes, our pastors blur the distinction between two unrelated issues (selfishness and marketplace work), but it's difficult not to fall into that trap when you preach to a congregation that spends more on dining out than on reaching the world's lost and dying.

---

10 David W. Miller, *God at Work*, 91.
11 Randy Alcorn, *The Treasure Principle* (Colorado Springs: Multnomah, 2001), 63.

Academic Influences

Throughout their training, some pastors are immersed in an anti-business atmosphere. Turning again to the survey statistics, we read, "The evidence suggests that the overarching presuppositions among theological faculty about capitalism, business, and marketplace issues range from indifference to negative. . . . Thus influenced by their faculty, the result is that seminary students' attitudes toward business . . . are 'overwhelmingly negative.'"[12]

I occasionally hang out with young pastors-in-training at Bible colleges and seminaries. Unfortunately, my experience lines up with the statistics. While talking with the young ministers, I'll often steer the conversation toward the marketplace. When I do, their words and attitudes sometimes become venomous and filled with self-regard for their own choice to rise above such sordidness. Some of our future shepherds appear to forget that their entire career will be paid for by regular, everyday people whose backs are bent in marketplace jobs.

Pastors often gain a much deeper perspective on other vocations after they spend a few years in the trenches of actual ministry. This may explain why some of the most ardent anti-business pastors are the young ones—straight out of seminary, preaching in jeans, ripping on the guitar during the worship set, raging against the stereotypical evils of the marketplace. True, their rants are based on a media-induced image of a corrupt business mogul, not the flesh-and-blood reality of the cost accountant sitting in cubicle 218E, but we should cut them some slack anyway. You and I would probably do the same thing if we were standing in their flip-flops.

---

[12] David W. Miller, *God at Work*, 97–98.

Subtractive versus Additive Outlooks

Another intriguing difference in perspectives is this: when it comes to economic needs, pastors are fundamentally subtractive in their outlook. The rest of us are additive. "For example, when asked about solutions for economic injustice," write Nash and McLennan, "the church frequently suggests giving away possessions and earnings, while businesspeople suggest creating more jobs. . . . One is a path of redistribution . . . the other is a path of creation."[13] The pastor hopes to divert resources from the marketplace; to him, less money in the hands of business means more money available for the needy and the church's capital campaign.

The pastor's subtractive economic approach initially seems to be more biblical. The theme *less is more* runs throughout the Bible. We empty ourselves of pride to find our greatest fulfillment in Christ. The last shall be first. It is better to give than receive. Blessed are the meek.[14] But if we rip these biblical truths out of context and haphazardly force-fit them to the marketplace, the marketplace would collapse. There would be no economy. There would be no businesses from which to *subtract* money for the needy and the church's capital campaign. We would be a society of hunter-gatherer scavengers.

The marketplace is additive; it must always be so. God designed it that way. "Be fruitful and multiply"[15] —flocks increased, cities multiplied, and nations emerged. God hardwired us to build, to add something to our place of work, to create economic gain. Years of education equip us for the task, and now we spend forty

---

13 Nash and McLennan, *Church on Sunday, Work on Monday,* 197.
14 Philippians 3:7–11, Matthew 20:16, Acts 20:35, Matthew 5:5
15 Genesis 1:28

(and sometimes eighty) hours a week working our tails off in order to be economically additive. Then we sit in a pew on Sunday morning and listen to thirty-five minutes of *subtract, subtract, subtract*—subtracting is more significant to God. Disconnect? Massive. Vocational guilt? Unbridled.

Both are correct. We need to create economic gain, and we need to give like crazy. The trouble comes when we latch on to only one side of the equation. The pastor operates in the nonprofit world. He lives on charity (redistribution), so his subtractive approach to money is understandable. But he creates an unnecessary disconnect between himself and his congregation when he implies that the marketplace is somehow bad or less significant because it pursues gain rather than redistribution. Let's acknowledge the view from his side of the pulpit. Then let's passionately give our money to causes that create sustainable solutions for the needy and carry the truth of Jesus Christ to unreached people throughout the world.

Differences in Personality

Differences in perspective are sometimes little more than basic differences in personality. Many pastors are inclined to contemplate problems at length; people in the marketplace are more apt to solve problems efficiently and decisively. Consequently, pastors can get frustrated by their members' *get-'er-done or get-out-of-the-way* attitudes. Meanwhile, churchgoers can get frustrated by the indecisiveness of pastors, especially when those pastors imply that a meandering, contemplative approach is godlier. Generally speaking, the luxury of extensive contemplation is only possible in the subsidized economy of the nonprofit world. In the business world—the world that generates the charitable funding for nonprofit organizations—such an approach typically would destroy a company's economic viability. Therefore, the pastor's implication rubs the tithing churchgoer raw.

Teaching Meat versus Milk

The practicality of sermons is often a point of disconnect. How much of your pastor's sermon is specifically applicable to the nuanced reality of your workday? Probably not much—at least, that's what it seems like. But we need to remember that the primary goal of preaching isn't to give us practical tips for the workday. The goal, rather, is to build in each of us a biblical worldview and a passion for Christ. In the long run, preaching with that intent will give us a stronger foundation for daily life and ultimately prove to be immensely practical. Additionally, it's impossible for pastors to custom-fit their sermons to each of our specific circumstances. Everything I'm writing in this section lumps all pastors into a single, sweeping, oversimplified generalization. Pastors are forced to do the same thing—generalize—when they talk about *our* jobs.

Yet our pastor's admonition to "do what Jesus would do" somehow loses traction in the middle of complex tradeoffs between short-term and long-term gains, bumping up headcount or requiring more overtime, laying off fifty employees or risking bankruptcy (and the ultimate loss of three hundred jobs), pocketing the per diem or turning in the actual expense receipts, tolerating chronic tardiness and team-demoralizing poor performance from an employee who is a single mother trying to support her family or firing her . . . *what exactly would Jesus do?* The workday is simply a lot messier than a sermon. And that's okay.

When we demand that our pastors deliver weekly sermons that are witty and full of practical nuggets of wisdom—nuggets we can put to immediate use in Monday's 8:30 a.m. production meeting—we abdicate our responsibility in the pastor-member relationship. We demand that the pastor feed us a baby bottle full of warm milk. But he's trying to serve up some thick T-bone steaks that were cooked over charcoal and sprinkled with Canadian Steak Seasoning. Applying the meat of God's Word to the complex reality of Monday morning is going to take some work and some teeth on our part. Pastors shouldn't have to serve us minced steak in a baby food jar. We need to pick up the knife and dig in.

Silence on the Topic of Work

When was the last time you heard a single sermon, let alone a series, that was focused on the topic of work—not a diatribe against the evils of the marketplace but a constructive message aimed at equipping us with a biblical perspective on the jobs we do and the challenges we face? Can't remember? Never? You're not alone.

Some of the confusion we experience in applying our faith to our work life is caused by the fact that pastors almost never talk about our work life—the activity that consumes the greatest portion of our waking hours. Disconnect? Yep.

This is part of the reason many Christians sit in pews and wonder why their hours of exhausting toil are apparently unworthy of being noticed by the church—or by God. In the words of one survey report, "[Churchgoers] go on separating their secular lives from their faith. . . . They do not find, nor seem to expect, much inspiration or guidance from the church at the most crucial level of their lives—where they carry out their daily work and influence."[16]

THE PROMISING TREND OF FAITH-AND-WORK INITIATIVES

Today, a growing number of pastors are recognizing the disconnect, and they're taking bold steps to overcome it. Faith-and-work initiatives are springing up in more and more churches as pastors seek ways to link our faith to our everyday working lives. These initiatives take many forms but generally are organized efforts of the church to actively celebrate the broad range of vocations represented within the community of believers, study and teach the rich biblical truths about work and vocation, and equip its members to live out their faith in the specific challenges they face at work.

Christian universities and seminaries are also beginning to take action. A growing number of them are establishing on-campus faith-and-work resource centers and study programs. The numbers are still relatively small, but the trend is promising. The church is beginning to take its own steps toward bridging the disconnect. However, we have a long way to go. Countless Christians still believe they are second-class citizens in the kingdom of God because they work in secular jobs. They still believe the lie of vocational guilt.

---

[16] "Listening-to-Lay People Project," quoted in Diehl, *Christianity and Real Life,* 19.

CHAPTER 4

GURU IN THE
MEANING-OF-WORK VOID

"The Power of Spirituality" . . . is arguably the
greatest megatrend in our era.

—Patricia Aburdene, author of *Megatrends*[1]

In today's workplace, it seems spirituality is anything that provides a higher meaning. . . . It can
be reading *Zen and the Art of Motorcycle Mainte-
nance* or religious fanaticism; transcendental meditation or communing with spirits; reading poetry
or Buddhism. Or none of the above.

—*Times of London*[2]

We believe that work isn't simply a paycheck; it is
the ultimate expression of a fully realized self.

—*Fast Company*[3]

---

[1] Patricia Aburdene, *Megatrends 2010: The Rise of Conscious Capitalism* (Charlottesville, VA:
Hampton Roads, 2007), xxi.

[2] Des Dearlove, "The Workplace Gets Spiritual," *The Times of London,* July 24, 2003 (accessed
July 14, 2011), http://business.timesonline.co.uk/tol/business/career_and_jobs/graduate_
management/article847676.ece.

[3] John A. Byrne, "The Promise of Reinvention," *Fast Company,* August 1, 2003 (accessed Janu-
ary 21, 2012), www.fastcompany.com/magazine/73/edlet.html.

The words echoing through the room demand a response. National leaders have never seen anything like it. A Senate subcommittee just heard testimony indicating that our country faces an unprecedented crisis—a looming national threat. Experts from Harvard and other leading institutions saw the shift more than a decade ago; analysts from the technology sector now confirm it. Top sociologists and national church councils are weighing in. The peril is undeniable. The United States must take action.

This isn't a scene from a movie in which we're about to be invaded by space aliens. Instead, this is a scene from history. The year was 1967. The looming crisis? You're not going to believe it, but the threat we faced was . . . *mass leisure.* Leisure? Yeah, you know—Sunday afternoon naps, eating barbecue at Henry's Smokehouse, and sitting around with neighbors on the front porch.

You see, in the 1950s and '60s, national forecasting experts predicted massive advances in technology. Consequently, there would be astronomical gains in workplace productivity. If that were to happen, then Americans could maintain their standard of living while reducing their work hours to only twenty-two hours a week, or we could all retire at age thirty-eight. That meant our nation would fundamentally shift from being a working society to a leisure society—a country stuck in constant *play* mode. This worried the experts, because it presented a massive social problem.

What would people do with all that free time? There would be millions of listless people lolling around, looking for something to do. Many experts feared the trouble that would inevitably arise from such widespread boredom. The crisis of mass leisure looked like a genuine, terrifying possibility.[4]

The truly amazing part of the story is that the experts were right on the mark. They nailed it when they predicted massive advances in technology and productivity. Between 1948 and 1991, productivity more than doubled. But what happened to our twenty-two-hour workweek or retirement at age thirty-eight? The experts missed one little detail that turned out to be the most important detail of all. They never imagined that by 1991, Americans would own and consume over twice as much as they did in 1948.[5] And in order to own and consume twice as much stuff, we would work twice as many hours. In a way, we did get the twenty-two-hour workweek, but we chose to double the amount of time we work each week. In the end, we landed right back at an average workweek of more than forty hours.

Our insatiable hunger to buy stuff literally outpaced our phenomenal gains in productivity. We chose to work more in order to consume more. The story is still the same today. In retrospect, the leisure crisis scare was more of a national joke rather than a national threat. A twenty-two-hour workweek? Retirement at thirty-eight? Not hardly. Instead, we experience grueling workweeks and an ever-increasing retirement age.

---

[4] See Nancy Gibbs, "How America Has Run Out of Time," *Time,* April 24, 1989 (accessed May 11, 2012), www.time.com/time/magazine/article/0,9171,957505-2,00.html; Russell Lynes, "Time On Our Hands," *Harpers,* July 1958, 34; and Juliet B. Schor, *The Overworked American: The Unexpected Decline of Leisure* (New York: Basic Books, 1993), 4.

[5] Schor, *The Overworked American,* 2.

Why do we wildly overwork and overspend? We could spend a lot of time and ink hashing out all the reasons, but let's just cut straight to the heart of it. We've swallowed a lie that says we *are* what we do, earn, wear, and own. More of everything means more of *me.* Consequently, our lives have become a frantic quest to earn and prove our worth—to know that we matter. *But it's exhausting!*

Work and the daily grind have spun out of control. We do more, spend more, own more, and work more than ever before. Our culture is collectively tired. The workday is hard enough. But then we go home and do even more work. We mow lawns, maintain cars, clean houses, iron clothes, cook dinner, change diapers, haul kids to innumerable sporting activities, pay bills, and then knock out a few e-mails before finally crashing. It's all grueling. People boil with tension, stress, anxiety, and road rage. Our schedules are overbooked, our responsibilities leave us overextended, and we are overwhelmed.

For many years, Western culture tried to mask the pain of stressful work and frazzled lives with the magical high of buying more stuff. Shopping seemed to be our national pastime. But today, that's changing. Sure, there will probably always be a huge segment of society that believes the lie that *you are what you earn, wear, and own,* but increasingly, modern people are finding that consumerism no longer tranquilizes the pain.

Five-adjective espresso drinks and nine-adjective luxury cars don't cut it anymore. Surveys repeatedly tell us that our increasing levels of consumption have failed to make us any happier. No kidding. We've known that for a long time, but today, we're beginning to do something about it. Now we're looking for something beyond a venti iced peppermint white chocolate mocha. We want the meaning of our work to be more eternal than a 3.0 liter, 6-

cylinder TwinPower, Turbotech, xDrive35i, intelligent all-wheel, X5 sport activity vehicle.

People are searching. They're stepping back and reevaluating their lives. They look at their demanding jobs, and what they see is a colossal void—an utter lack of meaning in the work they do all week long. They want something to replace the failed opiate of consumerism, something to fill the void and restore a sense of meaning to their lives and their work. Thus the search becomes a quest—often a spiritual quest.

People want to connect their work to who they are, and then they want to connect who they are to eternity—something that transcends time and lasts forever. We're no longer content to live divided lives in which our work selves are separate from our personal selves. Many of us—Christian and non-Christian alike—are looking for an answer that merges the secular and sacred sides of life. We want more than just a sliver of significance. We want meaning and eternal significance to infuse every moment and aspect of our lives.

It's important to note that most people do not necessarily seek to work fewer hours or spend less money. Rather, they look for something that will infuse daily life—which is mostly spent on the job—with transcendent meaning. Besides, working fewer hours isn't really an option for most of us. Go ahead; try to walk into the office tomorrow morning and tell your boss you've decided to work only twenty-two hours per week from now on. For most of us, that stunt would be an act of career suicide.

The reality of overhead costs and employee benefits packages means that it is usually cheaper to hire a few employees who work a ton of hours than to hire a lot of employees who work only a few hours. Consequently, our employment system has evolved into an all-or-nothing deal. We're told, in effect, "Take it or leave it. If you're not willing to put in the time, there's a long unemployment line full of highly-qualified people who are waiting to take your place—permanently." Long hours are a fact of life. Now we're on a quest to make eternal sense of those hours.

OUR CHANGING WORK WIDENS THE VOID

The meaning-of-work void isn't new. The author of Ecclesiastes wrote about it three thousand years ago. Today, however, the nature of our work is fundamentally changing; it is becoming more stressful and more abstract. In an information age, we increasingly work with our minds rather than our bodies. Our work is mentally exhausting and stressful rather than physically exhausting. We drag ourselves home with burned-out minds and souls instead of tired backs and biceps. With improved technology, even the tough jobs (construction, mining, farming, etc.) aren't nearly as tough as they used to be; they are becoming more dependent on the push of a button.

Today, many of us never see or truly comprehend the final product of our labor. Back in the old days, when we worked with our biceps, we could immediately see and touch the product of our labor. When we built a chair, we could sit in it. But now, when we upgrade some database software, the product of our effort is sort of hard to explain. Those who work in the manufacturing sector, a steadily declining sector in Western societies, face the same quandary. Manufacturing has become so specialized that many factories now produce unrecognizable components of who-knows-what. The component is shipped off to another factory—often on another continent—where it becomes part of a larger component, and so on. Factories rarely produce a finished product that you or I would recognize as something useful to life on this planet.

Even if we can actually see the product of our labor, many of us simply don't give a rip about it. Quarterly tax reports? Corrugated pipe? Rubber gaskets? An inventory analysis? This is not exactly the stuff of our childhood aspirations. When we labor to create stuff that is either inexplicable or mind-numbing, we often have no personal interest or emotional connection to the product of our labor; we tend to see our work as "just a job." The product itself is irrelevant; *it has nothing to do with who we are.*

From here, it's only a short slide into the abyss of meaninglessness. We battle rush-hour traffic on the way to stressful jobs where we produce abstract products that we couldn't care less about. Then, after an exhausting day, we drive home and wonder, *What's the point of it all? It's meaningless. My work—the very thing that consumes my peak energy and time, the task that dominates my life—is utterly meaningless. It has nothing to do with who I am, my faith, or God. It leaves no fingerprint on eternity.*

A DEADLY LIE STEPS INTO THE VOID

The changes taking place in modern work are triggering a tidal wave of everyday people who are setting out on a personal quest to fill the meaning-of-work void. For many, the quest soon becomes a spiritual quest. Our work, after all, is increasingly a function of our minds—our "inner spirits." There must be an answer somewhere. We turn to our churches, and we hear silence—or worse, we hear that we are wasting our lives in secular toil.

But in the local bookstore, at the company-sponsored motivational seminar, or in a magazine article, we discover a new message—one that embraces our working lives. It's powerful, and it's sweeping through offices all over the world. Many seek an answer to fill the void, and they find that answer not in the church, but in *modern spirituality.*

Definitions of modern spirituality are all over the map these days, so for the sake of our discussion, I define it here as an all-inclusive brew of New Age, Western, Eastern, and secular spiritualism plus a tiny dash of bloodless, noncommittal Christianity thrown in for good measure. Above all, modern spirituality is a lie that claims there are many paths to God. It defies the words of Jesus Christ: "I am the way, and the truth, and the life. No one comes to the Father except through me."[6] Yet today, for many people, modern spirituality is the lie that stands in the void.

SILENCE OF TRUTH

Winter is deadly here in the far north. It kills without mercy. We sometimes hear stories of it killing those who wander out into the cold and lose their way. When I consider the meaning-of-work void, I craft a similar story in my mind. I see the void as a story about a victim caught in a blizzard who dies only a few feet from the warmth and safety of her own home.

In the blinding wind and snow, the victim couldn't find her house. She didn't know the door was right in front of her. She was only a young child who had wandered outside. The house was full of people. Some sat around, playing cards in front of the fire. But

---

[6] John 14:6

nobody thought to go to the door and call for her. No one even noticed she was missing until it was too late.

No one knows what drew her out into the storm—probably concern for a pet. It doesn't really matter now; she's gone. In her confusion, she probably stumbled toward the tool shed, thinking it was home. But the shed is only a shell of a building with no heat or insulation, empty and cold inside; the wind cuts right through it. By the time she realized her mistake and turned back to search for the house, her energy was spent, and probably her hope, too. If only someone had opened the door and called for her. She was only a few feet away.

I talk with many Christians who grope around in the meaning-of-work void. Plagued by vocational guilt, they feel a total disconnect between their Sunday faith and the work they do Monday through Saturday. They search for an answer—something, anything that will give eternal meaning to their work. They tell me about their quest—their longing to find meaning in the void. As I listen, I can't help but think of that empty, cold shed. The image haunts me. In my mind, I see a sign nailed above the shed's door that reads *Modern Spirituality*. When I turn to look over at the house, I see a sign there, too: *The Church*.

Year after year, working Christians sit in pews and listen to the church devalue and marginalize their work. Ninety percent of their time and energy is trapped on the wrong side of the sacred-secular divide. Their calling in life seems to be lower rather than higher; their lifelong labor appears to have no eternal value. Few working Christians hear any message from the church that gives meaning to what they do all week long. Consequently, many of them begin to glance outside. They look out the window and think, *Maybe there's something else out there.*

There is—modern spirituality. It is a lie—a cold and empty shed—but there it stands, right in the middle of the void. It offers hope and answers custom-tailored to the working Christian; it takes the workplace seriously. Spiritual gurus promise eternal meaning to all of life. There is no sacred versus secular divide, higher or lower class system, or temporal futility. *Everything* is connected to the transcendent. With best-selling books, videos, articles, seminars, and a surging tide of cultural support, the guru provides the hope people seek. The everyday grit and exhausting grind of marketplace work is finally infused with spiritual meaning.

Working Christians are quietly slipping out the door, drawn outside by modern spirituality. Oh, sure, they still show up in a church pew each week. (After all, modern spirituality embraces *all* paths to transcendence.) But they've merged their Sunday faith with a lie that fills the weekday void. Their hearts have wandered outside. Nobody thought to go to the door and call for them. No one even noticed they were missing . . . until it was too late.

SEEKING MEANING FOR THE OTHER SIX DAYS

"Do you think I should go into the ministry?" That's the question I hear more than any other when I travel and speak in churches on the topic of missions. The person asking will often go on to say something like this: "I want to do something for God like you, but my work is just secular work. I design hydraulic hose fittings for a living. God doesn't need more hydraulic hose fittings. He needs more missionaries. Right?"

I've heard similar statements from pilots, bankers, heavy equipment operators, small business owners, and just about every other profession imaginable. Yes, God leads some of us into ministry jobs, and yes, I passionately believe we need more missionaries. But "my work is just secular work" is *not* a call into the ministry. That's the call of vocational guilt, not the call of God. The hydraulic hose fitting engineer and others like him are disillusioned because the church inadvertently—but consistently—implies that meaning and significance are only found in ministry activities, not in marketplace work.

Back at the office, however, modern spirituality offers an entirely different answer. Modern spirituality said to the church, "Fine, keep your Sunday. We'll take everything else—the other six days." Spirituality gurus, consultants, and coaches actively partner with the world's leading corporations. They use business-friendly language, and they offer a dazzling array of resources. The growth of spirituality in the workplace is commonly described as the Spirituality-in-Business Movement. Patricia Aburdene, author of the best-selling *Megatrends* books, states that spirituality "is arguably the greatest megatrend in our era."[7] Aburdene, herself a devotee of Spirit-in-Business, invites us along on a spiritual journey within a circle of like-minded followers:

> The coffee table, spread with power objects—beautiful fabrics, a large feather, sage and a giant shell—is transformed into an altar tonight, because Richard Whitely, sixty-four, one of our members, is taking us on a shamanistic journey to the underworld, where we'll meet power animals

---

[7] Aburdene, *Megatrends 2010*, xxi.

with powerful medicine to support our careers, work lives, and businesses.[8]

Those of us who trust in the God of the Bible should pause long and hard over that image, because that "journey to the underworld" is the answer standing in the void. It's no longer just a fringe, crystal-gazing attempt at escapism; it's not something to be ridiculed as the butt-end of clean Christian jokes. It is a growing wave of abandoned souls on a dead-earnest quest to bring eternal meaning into their regular, everyday work. And it's sweeping Christians away, too. Researchers Laura Nash and Scotty McLennan conclude:

> The absence of supportive church engagement in today's spiritual quest and the presence of many alternative spiritual expressions have posed deep problems for the businessperson and the Christian church. Already favoring syncretistic approaches to faith, [businesspeople] who cannot find any meaningful message on economic life in the church of their childhood look elsewhere to feed their spiritual hunger. Even businesspeople of deep Christian faith find it difficult to understand what Christianity has to say to their professional concerns.[9]

Many Christians feel that the church is totally irrelevant to the reality of Monday through Saturday. They respond to the silence in one of three ways. Many of them know modern spirituality is a

---

[8] Aburdene, *Megatrends 2010*, 79.
[9] Nash and McLennan, *Church on Sunday, Work on Monday*, xxv.

lie. It'll never lure them outside. But they feel abandoned in their quest to make eternal sense of the other six days. So they divide their lives, and then they struggle with a vague sense of guilt, wondering, *Am I wasting 90 percent of my life?* Others, however, merge their Christian faith with modern spirituality. They won't reject Christianity or the church, but they'll patch modern spirituality into all the gaps created by the church's silence. And for the millions of churchgoers who spend forty-plus hours a week grinding it out in the marketplace, those gaps add up to a massive void. Finally, a few will listen to the guru, and then they'll go all-in. Modern spirituality will become the core of their meaning and their hope for transcendent significance. They'll die only a few feet from the door of the church, lured outside by a lie that promised meaning to all of life, not just a sliver.

CULTURAL UNDERPINNINGS

How did modern spirituality surge into our workplaces, homes, media, and every other aspect of our modern lives? There are many reasons, but part of the answer can be given in just one word—Oprah. *Time.com* said she is "arguably the world's most powerful woman." *Forbes* magazine called her "the world's most powerful celebrity." *The American Spectator* reported, "Today she's arguably the most influential woman in the world."[10] Oprah superlatives fly off the pages of nearly every major publication. She

---

[10] *Time.com,* "Global Influentials: The Top 25 Business People Worldwide," December 2001 (accessed July 18, 2011), http://www.time.com/time/2001/influentials/; *BBC News,* "Oprah 'Most Powerful Celebrity'," June 14, 2007 (accessed February 15, 2012), http://news.bbc.co.uk/2/hi/entertainment/6753847.stm; John Tamny, "Embrace the Wealth Gap," *The American Spectator,* May 8, 2007 (accessed July 18, 2011), http://spectator.org/archives/2007/05/08/embrace-the-wealth-gap#.

even made *Life* magazine's list of 100 people who changed the world. Jesus made the list, too, along with Elvis.[11]

Back in 2002, *Christianity Today* said, "Oprah's most significant role has become that of spiritual leader. . . . She has become a postmodern priestess—an icon of church-free spirituality."[12] Modern spirituality has been gaining momentum for a long time, but before Oprah, it was still primarily relegated to the fringes of Western society. Then in the early 1990s, Oprah, *the most influential woman in the world,* threw the power of her influence behind modern spirituality. *Presto!* Spirituality went mainstream. As I type these words, Oprah's website *(www.oprah.com)* is open on my computer. The first topic I see, positioned directly beneath her photo, is "Spirit."

Today, the tidal wave of modern spirituality surging through our culture is big. It's even bigger than Oprah. We can't get enough of spiritually-conscious bestselling books, blockbuster movies, and TV shows. Angels, demons, the force, and harmony are huge commercial successes. We're awash with spiritual awareness. "Hey, have you downloaded the latest spirituality app for your handheld? You can use it to calculate your spiritual quotient score."

I staggered out of my study recently and headed toward the kitchen in search of coffee. On the way, I noticed that my kids were glued to the TV in our living room, so I paused to see what was so riveting. Misty, already on the scene and holding the TV remote, shot me a concerned glance. Within seconds, we heard child actors and space aliens call upon the energies of Jesus, Buddha,

---

[11] Robert Sullivan, ed., *LIFE 100 People Who Changed the World* (New York: Life Books, 2010), 14, 122, 126.

[12] LaTonya Taylor, "The Church of O," *Christianity Today,* April 1, 2002 (accessed July 18, 2011), http://www.christianitytoday.com/ct/2002/april1/1.38.html?start=2.

and our inner life force to help in the fight against evil. Quotes from Eastern mysticism and the Bible flowed together in a seamless essence. The forces of harmony appeared to be overcoming the forces of darkness, but suddenly, all was lost—the screen went blank. The force of Misty's thumb had overcome the force of the red power button on the remote.

INTANGIBLE ASSETS

When we're accustomed to the language of modern spirituality in our homes, it seems natural to hear it in our workplaces, too. Additionally, the way we do our work is changing, and those changes pave the way for modern spirituality to show up at our jobs. Here we will explore some of those changes. Keep in mind that modern spirituality does not cause the changes. It simply walks through the doors that were flung wide open by these changes—doors into our everyday working lives.

One of the biggest changes is the vanishing line between work life and home life. With web technology in the palm of our hands, nine-to-five is becoming twenty-four-seven. Now it's easy to get a little work done at dinner and between Little League innings. The rapid growth of mobile technology combined with our increasingly information-driven jobs means the line will continue to vanish over time.

We not only carry our work into our personal lives, but also carry our personal lives into our work. In the old days, people were supposed to leave their personal lives at the workplace door. Not anymore. Progressive companies provide services that take care of the whole person (at least until we get laid off, spun off, or downsized). Now the whole employee is invited through the workplace door—personal stuff and all.

Something unexpected happens when the line between work and personal life vanishes. Our corporate offices, job sites, and factory floors begin to feel like our families—or at least our primary places of community. Social scientists, political leaders, and religious leaders all generally agree that one of our primary needs is to feel like we're part of a community. Community and family are the two environments where we express our deepest feelings, hurts, hopes, and longings. They help us gain our sense of belonging and are often what people turn to when seeking to fulfill their God-given desire to be part of something bigger than themselves. But our sense of living in a close-knit neighborhood community began to disappear with the advent of the double-car attached garage and the TV. Urban sprawl swallows many small-town communities, and job relocations scatter the community of extended family to the four corners of the world. So where do increasing numbers of people turn for their sense of community? The workplace.

Citing the work of twelve leading thinkers, R. Paul Stevens summarizes what our workplaces are becoming:

> (1) The company is a community, not merely a corporation; it is a system for being, not merely a system for production and profit. (2) The new image of the manager is that of a spiritual elder caring for the souls of the employees. (3) Employees are members of the body working independently for the common good. (4) While mission statements, vision, goals and values will continue to *push* a company, a "higher purpose" (parallel to

the "Higher Power" made popular by Alcoholics Anonymous) will *pull* a company forward. (5) The corporation is an equipping (learning) organization that provides an environment for every-member service (ministry) so that each person will become more human, more creative and more integrated with the higher purpose.[13]

Corporations gain a competitive advantage when they foster a sense of community and offer resources to nurture the whole employee. This is why corporations increasingly fling their doors wide open to spirituality. The advantage hinges on an accounting concept called *intangible assets*. I just knocked the dust off of my Accounting 101 textbook, which says, "Intangible assets are assets which are used in the operation of the business but which have no physical substance."[14] In today's spiritually attuned culture, an asset that exists but has no physical substance sounds a lot like something that is *spiritual.*

Consider the key wealth-producing assets of modern first-world economies—intellectual property, brand identity, creative talent, managerial talent, employee intellect, and research and development. These are all *intangibles*—the products of human intelligence, skill, and emotion. The guru promises healthier minds and souls. Healthier minds and souls think more creatively, analyze more sharply, and lead more passionately. They produce better intangibles. Better intangibles produce better stock prices.

---

13 Paul R. Stevens and Robert Banks, eds., *The Marketplace Ministry Handbook: A Manual for Work, Money and Business* (Vancouver: Regent College, 2005), 164.
14 Robert F. Meigs and Walter B. Meigs, *Accounting: The Basis for Business Decisions* (New York: McGraw-Hill, 1990), 401.

Now we begin to see how modern spirituality landed in a gold mine when it stepped through the front doors of the workplace. It all comes together in the workplace. Work consumes the bulk of our hours. It takes our peak energy, creativity, and intellect. It determines our income and where we live. The workplace becomes our community and sometimes our family, and it is increasingly open to spiritual resources. Then along comes a guru with a message that makes perfect sense of it all and fits within the context and grit of everyday working reality. But where's the church? Where's the truth?

The silence of truth—the church's disinterest in the workplace—is a staggering missed opportunity to carry the only true source of hope into millions of seeking lives. These are the lives of everyday, hardworking people who are lost in the void, groping toward a cold and empty shed.

CHAPTER 5

MISCONCEPTIONS
ABOUT WORK

Misconception: Work Is a Curse

Misconception: Work Gives Us an Identity

Misconception: Our Paychecks Buy Us an Identity

Misconception: Worth = Vocational Esteem + Income

Misconception: It's Wrong to Desire Significance

We'll do some heavy lifting in this chapter. We will tackle five deeply rooted misconceptions about work. These misconceptions have been around for a long time. They're part of our culture, and they often show up in our churches. At various points in my life, I've wrestled with each of these misconceptions. Maybe you've wrestled with some or all of them, too. I invite you to join me in overcoming each of them with truths from the Bible. Additionally, the truths we'll discuss here are foundational to the rest of this book—and to life.

MISCONCEPTION: WORK IS A CURSE

You and I live in a fallen world. Blood, sweat, and tears define our working reality. Even if you love your job, there will always be particular moments and certain aspects of your job that are immensely frustrating. Innovation-crushing committees, mind-numbing compliance regulations, tyrannical bosses, dishonest employees, and belligerent clients are facts of life. They're like thorns and thistles in a farmer's field. And like those of the farmer, our boots slog through God-given earthly reality: "Cursed is the ground because of you; in pain you shall eat of it all the days of your life; thorns and thistles it shall bring forth for you; and you shall eat the plants of the field. By the sweat of your face you shall eat bread, till you return to the ground."[1]

Today, we battle against sin, death, and decay. We live and work *under* a curse, so it's easy to assume that work itself *is* a curse. But is it? In short, work is not a curse; it is "God's gift to man."[2] But many of us continue to believe that work is fundamentally a curse—a result of the fall of humankind. We assume we wouldn't have to work if Adam and Eve hadn't sinned back in the garden of Eden. But the Bible doesn't say that.

If Adam and Eve (and thereby, all people) had not fallen, we would still work in a vast array of jobs. However, our jobs wouldn't be plagued by frustrations and setbacks; they'd be unhindered joys. Work itself is not the curse. The curse is the frustration, decay, and futility that plague our work. In Part Two of this book, we will explore the blessing of work and the astonishing future in store for our labor. But for now, let's look at just two basic arguments as to why work is not a curse.

First, work is not a *result* of the curse. People worked *before* sin entered into the world. Work is part of the divine "very good." God worked to create the universe.[3] "And the capstone of that divine work," writes John Piper, "was man, a creature in God's own image designed to carry on the work of ruling and shaping and designing creation."[4] The Bible says God created humankind to subdue the earth, have dominion over it, and work the ground *before* the fall of humankind.[5] "The Lord God took the man and

---

[1] Genesis 3:17–19
[2] Ecclesiastes 3:13
[3] Genesis 2:2
[4] Piper, *Don't Waste Your Life*, 139.
[5] Genesis 1:26–29; 2:5, 15

put him in the garden of Eden to work it and keep it."[6] And then
God pronounced his sovereign decree over all creation: "Behold, it
was very good."[7] The first two chapters of Genesis clearly establish
humankind as workers, made in God's image, before the curse.

Second, our work was not the only thing put under the curse.
God also subjected childbearing to the curse—and having children
is not a curse. If we claim that work is a curse, then we must also
claim that having children is a curse. Many of us read Genesis
3:17–19, the "thorns and thistles" passage, and declare that work is
a curse. But I've never heard anyone read Genesis 3:16, the "pain
in childbearing" passage, and declare that having kids is a curse—
except for the time my five-year-old son painted the walls and
floor of our garage (and all the rain-soaked camping gear spread
out to dry inside of it) with a broom and a five-gallon bucket of
used motor oil. "Daddy, I painted for you."

The passages on work and childbearing are parallel. "To the
woman he said, 'I will surely multiply your pain in childbearing;
in pain you shall bring forth children.'"[8] Work is grueling. Childbearing is grueling. (At least, that was my distinct impression in
the delivery room with Misty.) Nevertheless, we tend to assume
work is a curse, and childbearing is a beautiful experience—a cele-
brated event that brings us adorable little pooping angels.

The issue boils down to this—work and childbearing are not
curses. Rather, they are cursed—cursed, not curses. Is this distinction hair-splitting? No, the difference is massive. The difference
between being *cursed* and being *a curse* is crucial. Jesus Christ is
the ultimate example. He was cursed on the cross when he bore

---

[6] Genesis 2:15
[7] Genesis 1:31
[8] Genesis 3:16

the infinite wrath of God for our sake, but he is not a curse. Likewise, work was cursed when Adam and Eve sinned, but work is not a curse.

You and I live in a time when much of our labor feels utterly meaningless, job security is sinking to an all-time low, and work-related anxiety is climbing to an all-time high. Our businesses fail, we get laid off, we sometimes have tyrannical bosses and dishonest employees, and occasionally, our five-year-old boys discover open buckets of used motor oil in the corner of the garage. But these things will not always be so. Long ago, before the fall of humankind, there was an unspoiled age. The day is coming when we will once again be free from thorns and thistles, sin, death, and decay. The day is coming when God will declare, "Behold, I am making all things new."[9]

MISCONCEPTION: WORK GIVES US AN IDENTITY

One of the first questions we ask when meeting someone new is, "What do you do for a living?" When they respond with "engineer," "CEO," "waitress," or "missionary," we tend to instantly label our new acquaintance with a prepackaged identity—a tidy set of assumptions about his or her education, social class, estimated net worth, and significance to God. We live in a culture that bases our individual identities, in large part, on our jobs. This is intriguing, because many people dislike or even hate their jobs.

---

[9] Revelation 21:5

A quick glance at survey statistics confirms what we already know. "Americans hate their jobs more than ever before in the past twenty years, with fewer than half saying they are satisfied."[10] Patrick Lencioni, author of the best-selling book, *The Three Signs of a Miserable Job,* writes, "It would be impossible to accurately measure the amount of misery in the workforce, but my experience tells me this: more people out there are miserable in their jobs than fulfilled by them."[11] That fact is not surprising. But now we have a problem. By anchoring our identity in our work, we trap ourselves in a dilemma: we are what we do, but many of us don't like what we do.

Even if we like our jobs, they can disappear overnight. Job security is a myth. Every morning, people get up and go to work only to discover that their jobs have vanished due to changing markets, advances in technology, fickle consumer preferences, or some other vagary of the marketplace. So now we have another dilemma: we are what we do, but what we do could vanish at any moment.

I grew up in the deep South, and there really was a kid in my neighborhood named Bubba. He was fourteen, two grades behind in school, and weighed nearly two hundred pounds. But even Bubba could have figured out that if we are what we don't like to do or what might vanish at any moment, then we have an honest-to-goodness identity crisis on our hands. Upon hearing about people in such a predicament, Bubba would've pondered things for a good, long time, all the while scratching his belly, before declaring, "Aw, heck, them's gotta be the stupiderist fools I ever knowed

---

[10] *MSNBC.com,* "Americans Hate Their Jobs More Than Ever," February 26, 2007 (accessed May 15, 2012), http://www.msnbc.msn.com/id/17348695/ns/business-careers/t/americans-hate-their-jobs-more-ever/.

[11] Patrick Lencioni, *The Three Signs of a Miserable Job* (San Francisco: Jossey-Bass, 2007), 219.

'bout." I think Bubba's assessment would be wiser than the theo-
ries of all the world's identity pundits combined. Sometimes I
wonder if God is thinking the same thing about us: "They anchor
their identities in their jobs? How dumb can they be?" Yet we do.
Many of us view our work as the defining factor of who and what
we are. The reason is simple.

We burn more time and energy at work than at anything else
we do in life by far. Our jobs, along with the daily grind of errands
and household chores, will consume the majority of the waking
hours in our adult lives. The hours consumed are not our second-
rate hours, but our prime hours—our highest energy, peak creativity, and sharpest intellect. Additionally, work strongly influences
(or flat-out determines) where we live. Thus it has a huge impact
on where we go to church, the friends we have, and the schools
our kids attend. There's simply no other activity that comes any-
where close to matching work's dominant influence over our lives.
Somewhere along the way, work becomes not only the dominant
influence, but also the defining identity of many of our lives.

In an effort to put the best possible spin on this reality, some
companies have turned to the magical wonder of titles. With the
stroke of a pen, we can paint impressive titles over ordinary jobs. A
title upgrade is a cheap way to reward employees with feelings of
self-esteem, status, and significance. The guy sitting in cubicle
218E is no longer just an accountant; he's the Senior Chief Executive Director of Budget Compliance and Cost Analysis. Have you
ever noticed that there are no longer any garbage men? Instead, we
have sanitation engineers. Whatever happened to janitors? Now
they're custodial technicians. Secretaries are administrative assis-
tants, salesmen are account executives, and it seems like almost
everyone at the bank got promoted to vice president. Studs Terkel

sums it up best: "A title, like clothes, may not make the man or woman, but it helps in the world of peers—and certainly impresses strangers. . . . At hospitals, the charming bill collector is called the patient's representative! It's a wonderland that Alice never envisioned."[12]

The gleam of a shiny title fades almost before the ink dries on our new business cards. We all know it's a game, yet we play it as if our identities depend on it. We hope it really means something to be called Senior Chief Executive Director. Our Human Resource departments can't keep pace; they can't invent new titles fast enough. The Human Resource Manager is now the Senior Chief Executive Director of Endlessly Creative Impressive Title Proliferation, because you and I desperately long to be somebody.

We all want an identity. We want to be unique and therefore significant in the grand scheme of things. We want to leave a mark on the world. But if our jobs and fancy titles aren't worthy of the task, then where else can we turn? Western culture is awash with this question. People search for an identity, but most of them look in all the wrong places. Strangely, most Christians do, too.

If we split our lives into sacred and secular, then each side of life needs an identity. The sacred sliver of life has its identity already. It's anchored in our faith or religion. But the secular bulk of life floats aimlessly adrift on a vast sea of identities. So we find modern people, Christian and non-Christian alike, looking here, there, and everywhere for *themselves*—their unique meaning, purpose, and significance.

---

[12] Terkel, *Working,* xvii.

MISCONCEPTION: OUR PAYCHECKS BUY US AN IDENTITY

The advertising industry is more than happy to offer us an identity with a price tag attached. But let's not be too quick to attack the ad industry with a barrage of churchy clichés. I'm a fan of good advertising. It's a superb tool for promoting good products and great ideas. However, when it steps across the line of integrity, advertising can be powerfully deceptive.

Advertising roots itself in answering the fundamental question, *Who am I?* Ads sell identity, plain and simple. They sell identity for one basic reason: we buy identity—ravenously. "Buy this gadget, car, boxer-brief, or shoe, and you, too, will be (fill in the blank with whatever identity you most desire—beautiful, wise, powerful, young, able to slam-dunk a basketball)."

Interestingly, advertising tinkers with identity in the everyday context of dishwashing soap, lawnmowers, computers, socks, and hair color—the stuff we produce at our jobs and buy with our paychecks. This is the earthy stuff that makes up 90 percent of our lives—the side of life that our churches almost never talk about. Advertising backfills a massive void of meaning and identity. It offers significance to the great bulk of life abandoned to languish on the secular side of the sacred-secular divide. Consequently, our credit card statements bulge with illusions of acquired identity—significance purchased on credit at an introductory 7.8% APR.

An Example of Buying an Identity

Misty and I, along with our five kids, live in a rugged little community situated on the edge of Wrangell-Saint Elias National Park, an ice-capped wilderness bigger than Switzerland and six times the size of Yellowstone. Everything about Wrangell-Saint Elias is massive and *fierce*. It is home to countless glaciers; raging, ice-choked rivers; and wave upon wave of colossal mountains, including nine of the sixteen highest peaks in North America. Few places in the world are more extreme, and few people are tougher than those who climb these mountains.

Locals around here know exactly the kind of iron body and chiseled heart it takes to scale these towering peaks, and they can spot a wannabe mountaineer from eighteen thousand feet. The wannabes look like they walked straight out of a trendy outdoor gear and clothing store—the kind of store where a middle-aged, out-of-shape guy can walk in feeling like a burned-out accountant, swipe his credit card, and walk out feeling like a mountain climber. It's the total image make-over and more: not only does the would-be climber sport the perfect mountaineering outfit, but he also has $4,000 of professional climbing equipment slung over his shoulder. He's all geared up, ready to climb Mt. Identity Crisis.

I recently stood in the checkout line of one of these stores and listened to the guy behind me who was buying a brand-new, $300 carbon ice axe. He monologued nonstop about his alleged climbing skills and upcoming summit attempts. His speech was appropriately sprinkled with impressive mountaineering terms. But one look at his soft hands and bulky midsection told me a different story. I could be totally wrong about the guy, but I bet he'd never spent a single minute of his life hanging from the end of an ice axe. What was he trying to prove?

To be fair, many amateur climbers buy expensive equipment and head to the backcountry for all sorts of good reasons. There's nothing wrong with enjoying our hobbies. But some of those amateur climbers look first and foremost for an identity. They're the ones I call *wannabes.* They want to be someone different than who they are at work every day. They view their work as merely a means to an end, a necessary evil. This is a tragic view of work, since they'll spend the largest portion of their waking hours working.

Wannabes buy all sorts of identities—not just mountain climbing. They dabble in photography, horse training, go-kart racing, and golf, too. For many of us, these hobbies are great challenges and just plain fun. Believe me, I've shanked buckets of golf balls deep into the woods with my insanely expensive set of custom-fitted irons. But for many people, these activities become *who they are.* Their nine-to-five jobs fail to give them a sense of identity, so they go shopping and strap on a whole new wannabe self. The guy in the checkout line is no longer the accountant whose hobby is mountain climbing. Instead, he's the mountain climber who does accounting to pay the bills. In the end, however, their wannabe identities will fail them—just like every other identity that is anchored in what we do, earn, wear, or own. "Will that be cash or credit for the carbon ice axe, sir?"

MISCONCEPTION: WORK IS THE FOUNDATION OF OUR WORTH

We can define this widely held misconception with a simple formula: our Worth = our Vocational Esteem + our Income.

Study that formula for a moment or two, and you'll discover that it's the encryption key to everything our culture believes about work. It unlocks the mystery behind the workaholic's toxic addiction. It explains, in part, the despair endured by the unemployed, and it reconciles our off-the-charts veneration of both Mother Teresa (penniless) and Bill Gates (billionaire). The formula is a monument to our culture's philosophy. It is unshakable in Western thought.

Let's first consider the paradox of Mother Teresa and Bill Gates. Mother Teresa was penniless, but she was a billionaire in terms of vocational esteem. It doesn't really matter where Bill lands on the scale of vocational esteem, because he's a billionaire in terms of US dollars. Either way, our culture idolizes them; they are among the gods and goddesses of contemporary history.

The formula plays out at every level of our culture. We can measure our worth by measuring our esteem or our income. And we'd better find a vocation that earns us one or the other or both, otherwise we're *worthless*. Is it any wonder that divorce courts, counseling centers, and late-night taverns all brim with workaholics? After all, if my worth is based on what I do, then I'm desperate to do more. I can never do enough. *The more I do, the more I earn; and the more I earn, the more I'm worth.* In time, some will gradually begin to equate their worth with who and what they are. Consequently, in their minds, *The more I earn, the more I am.*

In all honesty, workaholics get a bum rap. Sure, they've swallowed the formula's lie, but it's the lie we told them to swallow. They grew up being told, "Work hard; make a name for yourself; get out there, and make a killing." Well, they went out and did that. But then we suddenly turned the table on them. Now we condemn them for being derelict parents and neglectful spouses. Untold thousands of them will drown their confusion and despair in a liquor bottle. Meanwhile, the formula relentlessly whispers, *What you do determines who you are; what you do determines what you're worth.*

Taking a job in full-time Christian ministry is no escape. Workaholism hammers ministry guys, too. I don't have a rock-solid set of statistics in front of me, but after talking with many ministry leaders and staff members over the years, I'd bet my custom-fitted irons that the rate of workaholism in ministry is the same as the rate in most other vocations. Those in ministry are prone to focus on the esteem side of the formula: *the more I work, the more I am esteemed; and the more I am esteemed, the more I am.* We shouldn't be so surprised when the guy slumped over a drink at the bar has the worn-out title of "Reverend" in front of his name.

Finally, what does the formula imply about the unemployed, the elderly, and the disabled—those among us who have no income, and apparently, no vocational esteem? If the formula is true, then it shrieks a nightmarish accusation at them: *You are worthless! You are nothing!* It's no wonder so many who are unemployed struggle with a despairing sense of worthlessness. They believe our culture's formula for worth. Thus, they believe a relentless lie.

The Answer to Our Search for Identity and Worth

Work, income, vocational esteem, hobbies, impressive titles, fabulous clothing, gadgets, cars, boxer-briefs, and full-time ministry will all ultimately collapse under the weight of creating and sustaining our identities and our worth. Os Guinness, in his book *The Call,* shines some light on these empty shadows of identity and worth:

> Modern people are haunted by an inescapable question of biography: Who am I? From magazine covers to psychiatrists' couches to popular seminars, we are awash with self-styled answers to this question. But many people are dissatisfied with the answers peddled because they have a terrible deficiency: They don't explain what to each of us is the heart of our yearning—to know why we are each unique, utterly exceptional, and therefore significant as human beings.[13]

There is only one answer that goes to the heart of our yearning—Jesus Christ, the Holy Son of God. Our culture's formula for worth is not found in the Bible. Wait, I take that back—the Bible does talk about people who anchor their identity and worth in their vocational esteem, income, or any other fabricated illusion of significance. It says they are *fools.*[14]

We can do nothing to create or earn our true worth and eternal identity. God alone bestows on each of us a "unique, utterly

---

[13] Guinness, *The Call,* 20.
[14] Luke 12:20, 13:26–27; Matthew 6:19, 7:22–23

exceptional, and therefore significant"[15] identity—our name, our worth, the sum of who we are. Jesus Christ purchased our identity with his blood—our redemption as the sons and daughters of God. It's unfathomable. The Bible says God made us in his own image. Each of us is an exquisitely unique image bearer of the infinite God. We rebelled against our Maker, however, and became wretched slaves to sin and death, bound under the weight of our guilt and shame. But God sent us his Holy Son, "the firstborn of all creation,"[16] who paid the ultimate price to redeem our lives from bondage and destruction. Through the sacrifice of our Savior, God forgave us and adopted us as his own beloved sons and daughters—his heirs. Our everlasting Father laid his claim to us. We are his. That's who we are. That's our worth.

> God sent forth his Son, born of woman, born under the law, to redeem those who were under the law, so that we might receive adoption as sons. And because you are sons, God has sent the Spirit of his Son into our hearts, crying, "Abba! Father!" So you are no longer a slave, but a son, and if a son, then an heir through God. (Galatians 4:4–7)

This, our blood-bought identity, is a matchless gift, a priceless wonder. As such, it transcends all empty shadows of identity and worth—and it triumphs over the formula's lie. The vanquished formula gasps, *What you do and earn determines who you are.* But the Lord God of heaven and earth thunders, *What my Holy Son*

---

[15] Guinness, *The Call*, 20.
[16] Colossians 1:15

did and earned on the cross determines who you are! Your worth was purchased with his blood! You are mine!

MISCONCEPTION: IT'S WRONG TO DESIRE SIGNIFICANCE

Many of us struggle with a vague sense of guilt simply because, deep down, we really do want to be significant in the grand scheme of things. We want to be important, and since our work is a major part of our lives, we want it to be important, too. It feels like a hidden sin. We wonder, *Isn't the desire to be significant or to do significant work really just self-centered pride?* The short answer is no; the desire is a good desire that was built into us by God. He created us for a significance beyond anything we've ever dared to hope for. But at the same time, yes; you and I can twist our desire into the treasonous sin of pride. The desire itself, however, is not sin. It is good—very good.

The key to avoiding the empty misery of pride and finding mind-blowing significance is to lodge our God-given desire in the only true source of significance, God himself. However, if we don't know God, then we're left to search for significance in an endless maze of unfulfilling illusions. This quest is the engine that drives much of our modern culture. It's the desperate quest to be *somebody,* to be important, to be part of something big, and to be noticed by the world. A few years ago, I had an unexpected encounter with the quest that made me feel extremely small.

It was the middle of the night. My flight had just landed at Orlando International Airport. I flew in to spend a few days working with a large international organization. They had made all the travel arrangements and booked a room for me at some place called the Grand Bohemian Hotel. I'd never heard of the Grand Bohemian until I saw it printed on my travel itinerary, but my taxi driver's eyes widened a bit when I told him that's where I was headed. "Is it nice?" I asked.

The driver's reply percolated through a thick Haitian accent and a beaming grin. "Very nice, very nice . . . *big money.*" I was intrigued. Twenty minutes later, we slid into a lineup of limousines depositing guests at "big money." I opened the door of the taxicab, already feeling severely outclassed, and stepped into an all-out party scene of the rich and apparently famous. It was 1:00 a.m., but the Grand Bohemian was teeming with people and upscale energy. The drinks were flowing. The music was thumping. *The party was on.*

I noticed a lot of incredibly tall, athletic-looking men wearing very expensive . . . everything. They were surrounded by incredibly tall women who also wore very expensive everything. Gucci and Armani reigned as thread-gods of the hour. The whole scene was straight out of a fashion magazine, except for one glaring misfit—me, the rumpled guy standing there with a bewildered look on his face. A bellman snapped up my bags and whisked me up to my room. I asked, "What's going on?" His answer explained everything.

The NBA's Utah Jazz was in town, and the team members were my hotel mates for the next three days. At six foot two, I've never felt so small in all my life. Everything about the experience was big—big people, big diamonds, big tattoos, big money. All of it bigger than life—certainly bigger than my little life, and maybe bigger than yours, too.

The thing that intrigued me most about the whole experience was not the presence of basketball stars but the presence of starry-eyed fans. There they were, at 1:00 a.m., a small cluster of dedicated fans jostling for position behind barrier ropes outside the Grand Bohemian's lobby entrance—just ordinary people standing on the outside, looking in at the extraordinary. They pleaded for autographs by holding out official NBA team pictures and acid-free pens to anyone who walked through the doors. One of them, evidently nearsighted, held out a picture and pen to *me*. I felt like a superstar for about half a second. But then my fan grew suspicious and asked, "Hey, are you with the team?" I replied, "Uh, no, I'm just staying here. . . ." The picture and pen vanished.

Devoted fans pressed against those ropes day and night. They wanted to see inside the Bohemian—to catch a fleeting, split second of eye contact with something or someone bigger than life itself. Most of all, they yearned to be noticed, to be seen and valued by a real superstar—a living being so famous and powerful that he could spin the world on the tip of his finger.

At the very heart of sports mania and celebrity worship is the ultimate fan dream—the fantasy. We deeply yearn not only to be noticed, but somehow, against all odds, to also be invited in. Fans silently fantasize about being invited backstage, hanging out with the celebrities, and being part of the inner circle. They hope that someone magnificently powerful and famous will look into their eyes and say, "Come, follow me" and then invite them into a new, extraordinary life. Those NBA fans down in Orlando were longing, beyond all hope, to be personally invited into the Grand Bohemian and swept up into the larger-than-life party of money, fame, and stardom. They wanted to be part of something *big*. We all do.

We dream of being discovered by someone powerful. We imagine our lucky break when a megastar agent discovers our hidden talent, looks, or insight. And then, because of our newly discovered worth, he will invite us into the grand world of power and fame. We want to be part of something bigger than life. We're desperate to be significant.

Nameless people being discovered and catapulted to greatness is the stuff of legends and feel-good movies. This hope fuels our dreams and cranks up the Nielson ratings on shows like *American Idol,* the longest-running number-one show in the history of TV.

But when we step back and really think about it, the whole masquerade begins to feel a little bit silly. Middle-aged men and women going all gaga when a celebrity walks into the room? Adults with mortgages and minivans daydreaming about being swept up into the elite spheres of the big leagues or the big screen? Secretly yearning to be famous—seriously? It's absurd. Or is it?

Fame, in our culture, means significance. And significance, when it's all boiled down, is closely linked to duration of time. We want to do or be part of something that lasts a long time—or better yet, forever.

There's a fundamental link between value and duration. "A diamond is forever," according to the DeBeers Diamond Corporation; therefore, a diamond is valuable. Famous people endure. They leave a lasting mark on the world. They make a difference. We write books and make movies about their lives. The more famous they are, the longer they endure. Of course, the optimum fame would be fame that truly lasts forever. But imagine if someone could not only be famous forever, but also *live* forever. That would be the ultimate fame. That would be *eternal* significance.

Some argue that our desire for eternal significance is purely naive escapism—a pathetic diversion from the brutal reality of the daily grind. But what if our desire is really a shadow of something deeper? What if God planted this desperate hope deep within our hearts? For who but God could satisfy our yearning to be discovered and valued by someone supremely powerful? What if God designed us to be swept up into something unimaginably big—something so massive that it transcends time and the universe, something so important that it will last forever? What if God did all of that and called it *good?*

If God did all of that, then suddenly our ache for significance makes sense. Suddenly it's okay; we could even say it's virtuous. Here's the point I'm driving at: *God did do all of that!* The writer of Ecclesiastes tells us that God "has put eternity into man's heart."[17] From cover to cover, the Bible is rich with images of our spectacular place in eternity. God's message is clear. He made us to be immortal beings who are swept up into his great epic. He made us to be part of something that lasts forever. This has been his plan for us since before the foundation of the world[18] —since before he created human beings and pronounced his creation "very good."[19] Our desire for significance, at its core, is our God-given desire to be known and valued by him forevermore.

God installed our deep longing as an everlasting, God-oriented compass that always points toward our true home—eternity with him. God is the author of our longing, and he is its only satisfier. We bring absolutely nothing to the table, but we get *everything.* And in this stunning paradox, God is most glorified. Our ache for

---

[17] Ecclesiastes 3:11
[18] Ephesians 1:4–10
[19] Genesis 1:31

significance is the great yearning—the ultimate fantasy—that only he can fulfill.

The solution to avoiding a sense of guilt as well as pride isn't to desire less, it's to desire more! We must give full vent to our desire for significance and pursue it with abandon but pursue it in the right place and in the right Person. This is where we so easily get off track in our quest. Since the day sin entered the world, we've been spring-loaded to misplace our desire. It's exasperating! C. S. Lewis writes, "We are half-hearted creatures, fooling about with drink and sex and ambition when infinite joy is offered us, like an ignorant child who wants to go on making mud pies in a slum because he cannot imagine what is meant by the offer of a holiday at the sea. We are far too easily pleased."[20]

God planted a good and desperate longing deep inside of us, but we keep chasing after empty illusions. Take our infatuation with fame. We muck around in the mud-pie fantasy of adoring fans pleading for our autographs, but the Bible promises us a fame that shatters the boundaries of our imaginations. This is not a shallow fame conferred by fans lined up outside the Grand Bohemian, but an eternal fame conferred by God himself—God, the Maker of the universe, personally smiling on us and conferring on us what Lewis calls "the divine accolade,"[21] "Well done, good and faithful servant. You have been faithful over a little; I will set you over much."[22] And God's idea of "much" will simply blow our minds!

---

20 C. S. Lewis, *The Weight of Glory: And Other Addresses* (New York: HarperCollins, 2001), 26.
21 Lewis, *The Weight of Glory*, 36.
22 Matthew 25:21

———∞∞∞———

But we have a huge problem. How dare we hope for eternal significance when a glance at the aging face in the mirror screams at us, "You are dying"? It may be another five years or seventy-five years, but there's no escape—we're all dying, sooner or later. We seem to be trapped in a sick joke. How does the stench of death square with our God-given hunger for eternity? Our condition is absurd. And herein lies our great quandary. You and I long to put our mark on eternity. We privately ache to be recognized as an essential player in the game of the universe, but each of us careens toward a grimy little grave. We are walking worm food, longing for eternal life and worth.

It was not always this way. There was a time, long ago, when there was no death. Humans were once immortal. We walked in the presence of God, and we never doubted our worth to him— our true significance. But "sin came into the world through one man, and death through sin, and so death spread to all men."[23] Since that day, we have strained under the relentless curse of sin and death. We have forgotten our place with God—our true home and eternal destiny. But deep within, our pure and desperate yearning remains. It is a constant ache for things that once were and a longing hope for things yet to come. Lewis concludes:

> Apparently, then, our lifelong nostalgia, our longing to be reunited with something in the universe from which we now feel cut off, to be on the inside of some door which we have always seen from the outside, is no mere neurotic fancy, but the tru-

---

[23] Romans 5:12

est index of our real situation. And to be at last summoned inside would be both glory and honor beyond all our merits and also the healing of that old ache.[24]

The Master is working. Listen to his words, and you will hear the echo of a forging hammer. He is shaping the everlasting masterpiece of your life. The quandary of death leers at us, and yes, we are dying. But it will not always be so. The day is coming when we will be immortal once again. The barrier ropes of our great quandary will be pulled aside; the doors to eternity will swing wide open. Jesus Christ, the Holy Son of the Most High God, will look into our eyes and invite us inside. We follow him through life's veil of tears, and in the end, he will give us everything. He will sweep us up into his epic. Our significance is assured. It is breathtaking. It is eternal.

Following Jesus Christ is a leap of faith, but it is no blind leap. We're not left groping in the dark for a deity never seen or touched. We have grasped his hands; they bear unspeakable scars. At a particular moment in a specific place on our tiny little planet of rock and dirt, God opened a window in time and walked among us. On a hill just outside of Jerusalem, he purchased our eternal lives with his own life. His holy blood flowed through gaping wounds and soaked a Roman cross. He requires no blind leap. Instead, he reaches out his hand and summons us with the plain-spoken words, "Come, follow Me."[25] There can be no greater significance. Our quandary is solved. Forever.

---

[24] Lewis, *The Weight of Glory,* 42.
[25] Luke 18:22

PART TWO

THE TRUTH

CHAPTER 6

OUR BIOGRAPHY OF TRUST

I am telling you your story, not hers. No one is told any story but their own.

—Aslan, *The Chronicles of Narnia*[1]

I am God, and there is no other; I am God, and there is none like me, declaring the end from the beginning and from ancient times things not yet done, saying, "My counsel shall stand, and I will accomplish all my purpose," . . . I have spoken, and I will bring it to pass; I have purposed, and I will do it.

—Isaiah 46:9–11

Instead of comparing our lot with that of those who are more fortunate than we are, we should compare it with the lot of the great majority of our fellow men. It then appears that we are among the privileged.

—Helen Keller[2]

---

[1] C. S. Lewis, *The Horse and His Boy* (New York: HarperCollins, 1994), 202.
[2] Helen Keller, *The Open Door* (Garden City, NY: Doubleday, 1957), 34.

Click. In less than one hundredth of a second, the shutter of my camera captured an image that changed my life forever: the image of Third World poverty. She was seven or maybe eight years old, hungry, filthy, trudging barefoot through the raw sewage that littered the pathway. She gnawed on her fingers as she stared into the camera with dark, hollow eyes. Her entire universe was a cluster of mud huts clinging to the pitiful scrap of land that subsists between the Nile River and the encroaching desert sands of Egypt, and her name was Grace. Grace Awakened. I will never know her real, Egyptian fallahin name, but to me she will always be the image of God's grace—grace awakened in my heart for all eternity.

We were in our mid-twenties. Misty was full of vibrant life. I was full of . . . *myself.* As a new, overconfident MBA, I had just chalked up my first major business failure—an ill-conceived attempt to execute a less-than-friendly leveraged buyout of the company I worked for. The possibility that the deal might collapse and leave me stranded on the wrong end of a burned bridge never even crossed my invincible mind. I thought, *I'm about to take over this company; then I'll show 'em how to run a world-class business.* Oh yeah, I really showed them. My buyout attempt failed spectacularly. Then they fired me.

Bumming around as tourists for a few weeks in an exotic country like Egypt would be a perfect way for Misty and me to clear our heads and plan our next venture. But I was angry—angry at everyone, everything, and especially at God. *How could he turn his back on me and let that deal fall through? What kind of a God is he, anyway? It's unfair!* Then we saw Grace.

We saw thousands of fallahin peasants living in squalid conditions all along the Nile. They peddled their trinkets as we wandered through their villages, but none took any genuine interest in us. Then, in an instant, while I bellyached about God's unfairness to me, Grace appeared. Her eyes tore a hole through my heart—Misty's, too. She stood in the middle of that fetid path, staring into our eyes. As she stared, all the weight of undeserved, cosmic grace came crashing down on my wretched pride.

Her eyes demanded an answer to the question of our lives—the question you and I must each answer one day: Why was she born into squalid poverty—living in filth, tormented by disease and hunger—and not me? Why was I born to well-educated, healthy, American parents, while billions of people throughout the world cling to life on the edge of impoverishment? What exactly did I do to deserve the fabulous opportunity that comes with being born into a modern, first-world society? What great deed did I accomplish before I was conceived to earn such a rare gift? All of my anger over God's unfairness to me vanished. I lifted the camera, clicked a single photo, and then just stood there, speechless.

When Misty and I looked into the eyes of Grace, we looked into the perfect truth—the truth that we did absolutely nothing to deserve our lives of unfathomable luxury, freedom, and opportunity. Except for the unearned and undeserved grace of God, we should be standing there, barefoot, our feet covered with sewage. We must all, in the end, buckle under the weight of God's sovereign grace. Only God is God; there is no other.

For you formed my inward parts;
you knitted me together in my mother's womb.
I praise you, for I am fearfully and wonderfully made.
Wonderful are your works;
my soul knows it very well.
My frame was not hidden from you,
When I was being made in secret,
intricately woven in the depths of the earth.
Your eyes saw my unformed substance;
in your book were written, every one of them,
the days that were formed for me,
when as yet there was none of them.
How precious to me are your thoughts, O God!
How vast is the sum of them! (Psalm 139:13–17)

God's sovereign grace is the lens through which we begin to see the breathtaking truth about our lives, vocations, and eternal significance. It all starts with God, and it's all about him. "For who has known the mind of the Lord, or who has been his counselor? Or who has given a gift to him that he might be repaid? For from him and through him and to him are all things. To him be glory forever. Amen."[3]

When I listen to middle-class Americans lamenting their frustrating, mundane, seemingly meaningless work, I'm tempted to pull out a tattered photo of Grace. "Here, let's all stare at this while we complain about our jobs—the jobs that provide us with health insurance options, vacation time, and 401K retirement plans."

I know—I'm starting to sound a lot like Grandma: "Eat your broccoli, you little ingrates; there's millions of starving kids in Af-

---

[3] Romans 11:34–36

rica who'd be glad to eat it." But you have to admit that Grandma had a profound and overwhelming point. Millions of innocent people throughout the world go to jail or simply disappear. Millions of others have died in concentration camps and killing fields, and still millions more are murdered before they are born. Our sniveling, whining complaints about our work ring hollow in the ears of so many silent millions. At a minimum, our lives in Western society are a spectacular and rare gift of God's sovereign grace.

That photo of Grace hangs on my office wall. Next to it hangs an old photo taken decades ago. It's of a young boy who is playing with his favorite buddy—his pet dog. Like Grace, this little guy stares directly into the camera. But unlike Grace, his eyes are bright and blue. He is healthy, happy, and safe, grinning at the camera without a care in the world. The boy in the photo is me. The contrast between those two photos is staggering. The contrast is grace. Grace Awakened.

THE MYTH OF UNLIMITED CHOICE

"You can be anything you want to be." Okay, I want to be the starting point guard for the Utah Jazz. True, I have zero talent and only a twelve-inch vertical leap. But that's not a problem. I'll work out at the gym for the next three months while listening to the theme song from *Rocky III,* "Eye of the Tiger," at full volume. I'll run, jump, dribble, shoot, hire a personal trainer, get a big tattoo on my bicep, and train harder than any other NBA player in the world. When I step onto the court next season, they won't know what hit them. Look for me on TV during the season opener—but you'll have to squint your eyes and look really close. I'll be sitting in the nosebleed section with a bag of popcorn in my hands.

No matter how much I want it and no matter how hard I try, I'll never be an NBA basketball star. Yet our education system and most of our feel-good movies continually tell us, "You can be anything you want to be." That message is simply a load of hooey.

Long ago, very few people struggled with vocational guilt. They didn't wonder if their work mattered to God, and they certainly weren't concerned about missing their calling in life. The reason behind their stalwart sense of resolve was simple. They had no choice in what they did for a living. Choosing a different line of work was inconceivable. If there's no choice in the matter, then no one stresses out over the possibility of making the wrong choice. In his book *Beggar to King,* Walter Duckat profiles the everyday occupations of biblical times. He writes:

> Unlike today where the father may be a laborer and his son a distinguished scientist or industrial tycoon, in biblical times children naturally followed in the footsteps of their father. The entire idea of selecting an occupation on the basis of one's interests, abilities, or personality, which constitutes the approach of the modern vocational guidance movement, was unknown. Probably the only time when the son diverged from his father's occupation was when the latter became impoverished, a situation which commonly led to his and his son's enslavement.[4]

---

[4] Walter Duckat, *Beggar to King: All the Occupations of Biblical Times* (Garden City, NY: Doubleday & Company, 1968), xviii.

Choice is a modern, first-world novelty. Only a tiny fraction of humanity has ever enjoyed such a luxury. We get to choose our jobs, cars, toothpaste, and even our spouses. All these choices confront us with a dazzling array of options. But options cause stress—the stress of choosing correctly.

When I forget to take toothpaste with me on a trip, I sometimes get a tube from the hotel front desk. When I do, I don't have to worry about choosing the right brand of toothpaste, because there's usually only one complementary option—take it or leave it. I take it and don't think twice about it. By contrast, when we're grocery shopping and toothpaste is on the list, it's a whole different story. I stand before the Walmart toothpaste aisle, and despair grips me. I tremble in fear. The choices overwhelm me. I'm almost certainly going to blow it and get it all wrong. I collapse under the weight of the guilt—toothpaste guilt.

Likewise, the claim, "You can be anything you want to be" raises a series of complex problems. What exactly do I *want* to be? What *should* I be? What does God want me to be? We stand, bewildered, in front of the aisle of life's options, and despair grips us. This time, though, it's no joke. The confusion and guilt are devastating.

Things were simpler when, on your eighteenth birthday, your parents shoved you out into the world and said, "Here's your wife, here's your job, and here's your hut. Now get on with life." There was no choice in the matter; everything was decided for you. Your vocation was a function of where, when, and to whom you were born—a function of God's sovereign grace. But today, things are different. In the First World, we have unlimited choices. Or do we?

If we step back and seriously ponder our options, we begin to realize something that is slightly unnerving. When it comes to our vocational choices, we have very few options; unlimited choice is predominantly a myth. You and I may want to be NBA stars, astronauts, or archeologists, but what we can actually be is narrowly defined, mostly unchangeable, and almost entirely decided for us—a function of where, when, and to whom we were born. Yes, it's our responsibility to make wise choices within the array of options available to us, but we have very little choice over the dominant factors that shape our lives and determine our array of options. Instead, our vocations are almost entirely shaped by our DNA, community, family structure, college admissions policies, the economy, a couple of employment agencies, and possibly a free trade agreement with a country on the other side of the world.

Our vocation—the sum total of our work, roles, and relationships—is not something we choose from a boundless list of options. It is, rather, a gift of God's sovereign grace. Some may say, "But I want a different gift; I want to be the starting point guard, the CEO, the pastor." Others may feel their gift is an insignificant gift—a lesser or lower gift than another's. These are not trivial and inconsequential complaints; they are staggering accusations. And the plaintiffs should carefully weigh the merits of their case, for they bring cosmic charges against the Most High God, the sovereign King of kings and Lord of lords, our Creator and the Master of our fate. God is God, and there is no other.

Highly successful people do not owe their success to their own ambition. Instead, they owe it to "such things as their family, their birthplace, or even their birth date," writes Malcolm Gladwell in his bestselling book, *Outliers*. Near the end of the book, he concludes, "Success follows a predictable course. It is not the brightest who succeed. . . . Nor is success simply the sum of the decisions and efforts we make on our own behalf. It is, rather, a gift."[5]

Throughout human history, untold multitudes of intelligent people have made wise choices and worked their fingers to the bone—and then starved to death. By all standards of human history, those of us who live in modern Western societies lead fabulously opulent lives. When we comprehend the rarity of our privileged existence, we begin to grasp the implication of God's sovereign grace, and it annihilates our wretched pride. My vocation, life, and privileged existence are astonishing, undeserved gifts from God. My biography is his. Yours is, too.

But what about Grace, the fallahin peasant—is her biography God's? As easily as you and I could have been born into squalid poverty, she could have been born into opulent luxury. Yet God, in his wisdom, did not will it so. He gave her a different story, her very own place to shape the masterpiece of eternity. Her biography is also his. As such, Grace, the fallahin peasant, is no less significant to God than Paul, the corporate finance guy. The significance of our lives is vested in the giver of our lives. Therefore, a Haitian immigrant taxi driver is no less significant to God than an American overseas missionary, and a truck driver is no less significant to God than an assistant pastor. Our biographies are all his. Horace Bushnell,[6] nineteenth-century pastor and author, wrote:

> Every human soul has a complete and perfect plan, cherished for it in the heart of God—a divine biography marked out, which it enters into

---

5 Malcolm Gladwell, *Outliers: The Story of Success* (New York: Little, Brown and Company, 2008), 267.

6 Whereas some of Bushnell's theology is in error, particularly his theory of the atonement, he gets it right in his understanding of God's pervasive and absolute guiding hand in our lives.

life, to live. This life, rightly unfolded, will be a complete and beautiful whole, an experience led on by God . . . a drama cast in the mould of a perfect art, with no part wanting; a divine study . . . that shall forever unfold, in wondrous beauty, the love and faithfulness of God; great in its conception, great in the Divine skill by which it is shaped. . . . We live in the Divine thought. We fill a place in the great everlasting plan of God's intelligence. We never sink below his care, never drop out of his counsel.[7]

We can't be anything we want to be. We can, rather, be exactly what God made us to be. This is not fatalism, but hope. We are in an epic battle. Those who are strong must fight for the weak. We must fight for Grace and the poverty-stricken masses just like her. Doing our part to relieve our fellow humankind of suffering is an essential aspect of our God-given duty and task. We fight not in the despair of fatalistic defeat but in the hope of God's sovereign promise of victory. We each have our own place to stand and fight—our own story to live. The eternal significance of each of our lives, whether peasant or taxi driver or pastor, is breathtaking. The author of each is God, the sovereign Lord of all.

DISCOVERING OUR CALLING WITHOUT GUILT

Our particular calling in life is the thing God put us on this earth to do. We often describe it as our career choice, or more broadly

---

[7] Horace Bushnell, *Sermons for the New Life,* Centenary Edition (New York: Charles Scribner's Sons, 1904), 14.

(and more accurately), as our vocation—the sum total of life's work, roles, and relationships. It's the answer to the question, *What does God want me to do with my life?*

For many Christians, discovering that answer is an enterprise fraught with confusion, fear, and guilt. They view life as if it were a big test—a single shot at discovering God's perfect plan. Getting the answer wrong means flunking the test and winding up in the cheap seats of eternal significance. It's no wonder people are desperate to discern God's calling for their lives. They agonize over the uncertainty, and they grasp at anything promising to unlock the mystery. Books, seminars, Bible studies—anything dealing with the topic is popular today.

There are two aspects of calling: the big picture (our *primary* calling) and the details (our *particular* calling). From a big-picture perspective, there's no mystery about God's calling for our lives. The Bible tells us that he explicitly calls us to himself with the plainspoken words, "follow me,"[8] and then he says, "Be holy, for I am holy."[9] It's simple—we must follow God and be perfect in everything we do. That's his explicit will for each of us. Great, thanks. Are you discouraged yet? You're not alone; all of us blow it every single day of our lives.

Further discussion about the specific details of our calling is pointless unless we first solve the underlying problem of God's holiness and our failure to measure up to it. The good news is that God has already solved the problem. He sent his Son, Jesus Christ, to live a perfect life and then die in our place. When we stand before God and give an account of our lives, we won't point to our own accomplishments; we'll point to his. Jesus' perfection merits

---

[8] John 21:22
[9] Leviticus 11:44, 20:7; 1 Peter 1:15

our eternal significance, not ours. And he bestows it on us freely; we merely accept it in wonder and awe.

The process of discovering the specific details of our calling must always begin at the foundation of Jesus Christ. He purchased our everlasting lives with his own blood. His sacrifice decimates the underlying premise of all sacred-secular, higher-lower, dualistic formulations of significance and calling. Two-tier systems all imply we can earn our significance by doing something *for* God. But we cannot. We cannot earn our significance, and we cannot do anything for God. This is the point where countless Christians go wildly off course in their effort to discover their calling.

The belief that we can do something *for* God in order to become more significant *to* God is a subtle but toxic lie. It poisons thousands of Christians with false guilt, and it drives some of them into ministry positions for which they are unskilled and ill-equipped. They equate significance with doing something for God, and then they define "doing something for God" as a career in Christian ministry. All other careers are lower, inconsequential calls—God's second best. Oswald Chambers writes, "The greatest competitor of devotion to Jesus is service for Him. . . . The one aim of the call of God is the satisfaction of God, not a call to do something for Him."[10]

God is not a cliché. He is the great I AM—the Almighty. He is the sovereign Creator of all life and matter. You and I are tiny products of his creation; "in him we live and move and have our being."[11] He does exactly what he wants to do exactly when he wants to do it. At this instant, he is orchestrating trillions of subatomic systems that keep our bodies from suddenly vaporizing. At

---

[10] Chambers, *My Utmost for His Highest,* 13.
[11] Acts 17:28

the same time, he sustains the atomic structures of over two hundred billion distant galaxies. Any notion that you and I can somehow do something for God or impress him is worse than stupid; it's blasphemous. We don't work for God. Instead, God works in and through us. Our task is to worship him with every second of our lives and to reflect his glory wherever he leads us, whether that's in a pulpit or on the deck of a commercial fishing vessel.

But what exactly does God want me to do? Where precisely is he leading me? Which is it—the pulpit or the sea, or something else altogether? Even when we are free from the lie of the sacred-secular divide, we struggle with uncertainty and guilt over our inability to conclusively discern God's specific, detailed plan for our lives. *What should I major in at college? Which job offer should I accept?* The wave of anxiety associated with failing to discern God's perfect plan is totally unnecessary. It is rooted in the notion that we have to get it exactly right, because the significance of our lives depends on it. We perpetuate this unnecessary guilt with questions like, "Are you in the center of God's perfect will for your life? Have you settled for God's second best? Are you obeying the still, small voice of God?" Let's shine the light of truth into this fog of confusion.

The Truth about Levels of "Best"

So, you loved art, and you were good at it. But you majored in accounting, because you thought it would be a more lucrative career. Yep, you missed it—you missed God's will for your life. You blew it when you were eighteen. But does that mean God downgraded your eternal significance by a level? Are you now stuck in the ranks of God's second best? Oh, but then there was that time you moved your family across the country against the advice of every sane person you know to take a job with a company that went bankrupt the day after you arrived. You missed it again. Are you now downgraded to God's third best, another level lower on the significance scale? Are you living his "Plan C" for your life?

When will it ever end? If each mistake knocks us down one more level of God's best, then by the time we're forty years old, we're somewhere around God's 1,768th best. We're hopeless. But in the Bible, we read about great people like Abraham, Sarah, Moses, Rahab, Elijah, David, Paul, Peter, and others whose lives were filled with blunders. When confronted with important decisions, they often missed God's will for their lives. But in the end, they wound up exactly where God wanted them to be, and now God holds them up to us as examples of faith.

God does not throw his hands up in divine exasperation, and he doesn't downgrade us by yet another level each time we fail to get our calling right. Such a god is not the infinite God of the Bible. Such a god is a god of despair and guilt, not of hope. God is not derailed by our failure to discern or follow his calling. "And we know that for those who love God all things work together for good"[12]—even our blunders.

The Truth about the Still, Small Voice

When Christians talk about discovering God's call, they often mention the mysterious "still, small voice of God." But ask them what exactly they mean by it, and you get answers like, "a feeling," "a hunch," "a sense," or "an inner impression." These answers are

[12] Romans 8:28

intriguing, but how do any of them give us absolute clarity on God's specific, detailed plan for our lives when we're deciding on a college major, a spouse, or a career path? Those feelings, hunches, senses, and impressions all seem to change a lot.

Many people imply that hearing the still, small voice of God is an essential means of discerning God's will. But how many Christians actually hear it—I mean *really* hear it? The problem is that if we create an expectation that discovering God's will involves hearing a mysterious voice from God, whether an inner voice or an audible voice, then we inflict false guilt on millions of Christians. No matter how much they pray and carefully listen, most people simply can't be absolutely certain they hear it. Sure, they experience some feelings, but are those feelings the voice of God, just human emotions, or the result of low blood sugar? The uncertainty gnaws at the hearts and minds of those who are desperate to hear and obey the voice of God.

Measuring someone's ability to know God's will by their ability to discern a mysterious voice or an inner impression is an affront to the Word of God. Nowhere in the Bible do we find a still, small voice—at least, not one that is barely discernible and rarely explicit but nevertheless our pathway to discerning God's plan for our lives. The only way we could conjure up such a notion is to rip 1 Kings 19:12 completely out of context and thereby twist the entire meaning of the passage.

Here's the scene: Elijah was already in the middle of a conversation with the Lord about the dramatic struggle going on in Israel, and the Lord said to him, "Okay, Elijah, listen up here. I'm going to tell you something really important. I'm going to tell you the game plan. But just to make sure I have your undivided attention, I want you to go out there and stand on the mountain before me . . . and watch this!"

> And he said, "Go out and stand on the mount before the Lord." And behold, the Lord passed by, and a great and strong wind tore the mountains and broke in pieces the rocks before the Lord, but the Lord was not in the wind. And after the wind an earthquake, but the Lord was not in the earthquake. And after the earthquake a fire, but the Lord was not in the fire. And after the fire the sound of a low whisper. And when Elijah heard it, he wrapped his face in his cloak and went out and stood at the entrance of the cave. And behold, there came a voice to him and said . . . (1 Kings 19:11–13)

"Do I have your full attention now, Elijah? Okay, listen up; here's what I want you to do. . . ." And then the Lord told Elijah the explicit details of the game plan.

The King James Version of the Bible translates the phrase "sound of a low whisper" as "a still, small voice." This is where the term originated. Other translations call it "a sound of gentle blowing" or "a sound of sheer silence." But no matter how it is translated, we can see from the text that this sound is not the same thing as the voice of God. The voice of God came to Elijah *after* he heard "the sound of a low whisper." Additionally, if we continue reading the passage, we see that the voice of God told Elijah explicitly clear details of what to do next. These details included specific names, places, events, task assignments, job titles, succession plans, and quantities.

The still, small voice so many have strained to hear all their lives was the explicitly clear command of the Lord—not just a vague feeling—that came on the backdraft of a fire and was preceded by an earthquake that was preceded by a strong wind that tore the mountains and broke the rocks into pieces!

The wind, earthquake, and fire are like a great symphony building to a deafening climax. Then, just after the thundering peak, the music pauses in total silence. Every ear waits, rapt with anticipation. At last, out of that breathless silence, soars a single, clear, piercing, unforgettable note—the voice of God.

Imagine Elijah standing on the side of that mountain. I can't picture him nervously wondering, *Was that it? Was that the still, small voice of God? I just want to be sure; it's so hard to tell—to be absolutely certain. I'd hate to get it all wrong and miss God's will for my life. Maybe I should attend another seminar on discerning the voice of God.* Meanwhile, many of us feel guilty, because we've been taught that being in the center of God's will means obeying his still, small voice. Yet no matter how hard we try, we don't seem to be spiritual enough to discern it confidently. That guilt is nonsense; it is simply a lie.

God does not play cruel little games, taunting us with his plan while holding it just out of reach, veiled in the mystery of a still, small voice. The God who *spoke* the universe into existence is perfectly capable of telling you and me, in explicit detail, what to do in any given situation. If he wants us to know something, we will know it—absolutely and without any doubt. We couldn't possibly miss it. He can speak to us with his voice, an earthquake, fire, or his written Word. The key is this: hearing a faint, barely discernible, still, small voice can never be a prerequisite for discovering our calling.

THE FUTURE BELONGS TO GOD

I've strapped on a backpack and climbed many mountains over the years. While up there, I've often prayed for God's wisdom and leading in my life. But I feel totally ripped off: not once has God ever said, "Hey, Paul, watch this," and then shredded the mountains with wind and fire before telling me exactly what to do with the rest of my life. How about you? It'd be awesome to have it all spelled out for us like that; we'd never wonder if we missed God's calling for our lives. But God in his wisdom doesn't speak to us that way these days—at least, not to anyone I've ever met. He could, though. I wish he would, just like he did back in the old days.

God used a talking donkey to get Balaam's attention, the apostle Paul saw a blinding light, and God spoke to Moses from out of the burning bush. If you walk into your office tomorrow morning, your desk suddenly bursts into flames, and God speaks to you from the midst of it, then you'd better do exactly what he says! But if God chooses not to spell out the step-by-step game plan for our lives, then we have absolutely no right to wallow in despair, frustration, and guilt. The future is his alone, and the choice not to reveal that future is also his alone. To demand otherwise of him is presumptuous arrogance on our part. John Piper writes:

> God does not intend for us to know most of his sovereign will ahead of time. "The secret things belong to the Lord our God, but the things that are revealed belong to us" (Deuteronomy 29:29). If you want to know the future details of God's will of decree, you don't want a renewed mind,

you want a crystal ball. This is not called transformation and obedience; it's called divination, soothsaying.[13]

So how do we decide between a college major in art or accounting, between accepting the job offer in Phoenix or the one in Atlanta, or between working for a nonprofit ministry or a for-profit business? After all, in today's world of possibilities, these are decisions we must occasionally make. Never fear; an entire industry has sprung up to save the day and relieve us of our anxiety—the Christian vocational guidance industry. Today there are countless books, seminars, Bible studies, and ministries dedicated to helping us understand God's true calling for our lives. Many of these resources are excellent. Some are revolting.

Any book or ministry that advocates the pursuit of personal wealth as the key to discovering your calling—as in, "God wants you to be rich, so go for the money"—is a load of malarkey. Ignore it. The same is true of any resource that insists our calling is only discovered through signs, wonders, visions, or dreams. You may experience signs, wonders, visions, and dreams, but these are not a prerequisite to knowing the will of God. Organizations that promote regular quiet times of spiritual retreat and discernment are closer to the mark. But let's make sure we fill our minds with the wisdom and truth of the written Word of God during those retreats as opposed to emptying our minds and waiting for a sign or a voice.

---

[13] John Piper, "What Is the Will of God and How Do We Know It?" August 22, 2004 (accessed February 10, 2011), http://www.desiringgod.org/resource-library/sermons/what-is-the-will-of-god-and-how-do-we-know-it.

The best vocational guidance books and ministries are those that aim to saturate our minds with the Word of God and then they help us assess our own unique, God-given shape. Our callings are often written in our gifts (our abilities, talents, personalities, and heartfelt passions). Rick Warren, author of *The Purpose Driven Life,* writes, "Before God created you, he decided what role he wanted you to play on earth. He planned exactly how he wanted you to serve him, and then he shaped you for those tasks."[14]

The underlying premise of this model is that by identifying our gifts, we can identify God's calling for our lives (or at least narrow down the options). I have the musical talent of a brick, and opera gives me migraines. Singing opera is probably not my calling (unless God speaks to me from out of my burning desk and tells me otherwise). This approach to discovering our calling is excellent, and I recommend it wholeheartedly. There is, however, one place where this approach consistently runs into deep trouble—real life.

THE TROUBLE WITH GIFTS TESTS

Gifts tests are all the rage these days. They're designed to help us discover our abilities, talents, personalities, passions, and spiritual gifts. Career guidance coaches tell us we can discover our specific, God-given calling by discovering our specific, God-given gifts. First, we take a gifts test, which helps us understand what we're good at and what we love to do. Then we find a job that fits those gifts and interests. It's simple. Find a job doing something you're

---

[14] Rick Warren, *The Purpose Driven Life: What On Earth Am I Here For?* (Grand Rapids: Zondervan, 2002), 234.

good at and love to do, and wonder of wonders, you'll love it and be good at it. The unspoken assumption seems to be that loving your job, apparently, is the best indication that you are in the center of God's will for your life. But we have a problem. We can hear it in this comment from a guy who recently attended a church-sponsored "discover your calling" seminar: "The seminar was excellent—high-energy speaker, dynamic video clips. The whole idea of discovering our calling in our gifts and passions really hit home with everyone. The event would have been very helpful back when I was eighteen. But now I'm forty-three and trapped. I missed God's call for my life a long time ago." This was shared by an accountant (who should have been an artist).

In *The Purpose Driven Life,* Rick Warren writes, "Figure out what you love to do—what God gave you a heart to do—and then do it for his glory."[15] This is excellent career guidance advice. But for most of us, it's a pipe dream—a dream that inflicts a ton of guilt when it slams into the reality of our limited options. When we read materials or listen to speakers who teach the gifts-based approach to discovering our calling, we often see or hear statements similar to the following: "God never wastes the abilities he gave you. He would not give you interests, talents, and personalities unless he planned to use them for his glory. By identifying these gifts, you can discover God's will for your life."

Initially, that statement seems to make a lot of sense. But what does it say to the forty-three-year-old accountant—the one who is essentially locked out of a career that lines up with his gifts and passions? What does it say to Grace, the Egyptian fallahin peasant? And what does it say to billions of people who have no choice in

---

15 Warren, *The Purpose Driven Life,* 239.

what they do to survive day by day? That statement excludes the world's masses from any possibility of being in God's will for their lives. And it screams the lie of guilt: *You have failed to be what God made you to be; you've blown God's perfect plan. Your life is a waste of good gifts.*

It is likely that the greatest painter who ever lived never painted, the most talented musician never played a single note, the greatest mathematician never learned to multiply, and the greatest writer never learned to read. They possibly died, never even knowing the depth and riches of their God-given talent. They either slogged through a life of peasant survival or starved to death at an early age. Perhaps they were aborted. We don't even know their names—but we will. The day is coming when their gifts will blaze forth and glorify God for all eternity. That day, though, is not today. Today we live in a world that is fallen—a world at war.

Gifts tests have their place, but they become a scourge of guilt when we presume that God will conform his sovereign will to our perceived best use of those gifts. The tabulated results of a gifts test do not trump God's sovereign providence. God is God—Lord and Master over every aspect of our lives, not just our gifts. Os Guinness writes, "It is wrong to treat God as a grand employment agency, a celestial executive searcher to find perfect fits for our perfect gifts. The truth is not that God is finding us a place for our gifts but that God has created us and our gifts for a place of his choosing."[16] That place, for most Christians, is not in the center of their gifts. There is far more to God's calling than a simple career choice based on what we're good at and love to do. God's calling

---

16 Guinness, *The Call,* 46.

for our lives encompasses all of life; it is our God-given vocation, our divine biography.

The statement is absolutely true—God never wastes our gifts, and he plans to use them for his glory. The only question is, *When?* None of us have ever seen more than a fleeting glimpse of the breathtaking potential locked within our gifts, nor will we in this fallen world. But the day is coming when we will each see the giver of our gifts face-to-face. Then we will experience the mind-blowing, unimpeded actualization of those gifts. On that day, we will at last fully realize that our biographies were secure in the sovereign hand of God all along.

Today, however, in a world of thorns and thistles, the opportunity to make career choices according to our gifts is spectacularly rare. It is beyond the realm of possibility for all but the tiniest fraction of humanity. It is an undeserved and unearned blessing of God's sovereign grace. By all means, those of us who were given this blessing of opportunity should sign up for the seminars and take the gifts tests. Whenever possible, we should choose jobs that fit our gifts and passions. While we're at it, let's do a better job of teaching our eighteen-year-olds to do the same.

But we must never allow the shadow of vocational guilt to creep into our lives when we find ourselves in jobs that don't fit us. God knows your name and mine, and he knows our plight. The sovereign God of the universe doesn't lose track of us among the billions, and his sovereign will isn't knocked off balance by our stupid choices at eighteen—or forty-three. He isn't thwarted by economic downturns, changes in national trade policy, or technology-driven job obsolescence. He alone is God, Creator of the universe. "He does according to his will among the host of heaven and among the inhabitants of the earth; and none can stay his hand."[17] Our unique biographies rest in that very same hand—the hand that authors our lives.

ULTIMATE TRUST

Read a hundred books on discerning your calling, attend a dozen seminars, exhaust every recommended six-step plan, take every gifts test offered, ask your pastor's advice, spend a week in a cave praying for discernment, and after all this, in the end, God usually chooses not to tell us the specific game plan for our lives. He doesn't swoop down in a fiery cloud and explicitly tell us what to do in life's pivotal decisions. He doesn't tell us what to study in college or whether to accept the job offer in Phoenix or the one in Atlanta. He leaves us grappling with uncertainty. When the time for consideration is over and we must make our decisions, we're never quite 100 percent sure. We're mostly sure, but there's always a familiar, lingering thread of doubt. So we take a deep breath, check the box, and send the e-mail. Then we quietly wonder—sometimes for a lifetime—*Did I make the right choice? Was that God's perfect will for my life?*

There's an eternal, supreme purpose to the ambiguous tension of our lives. Buried in the heart of each decision's uncertainty lies a deeper, all-consuming question—the question of our eternal destiny. It is God's ultimate question to us: "Do you trust me?" You and I simply do not know all the details of God's sovereign plan. Will we trust God, the Almighty Father, Maker of heaven and earth, with our biographies? To trust is to plant our boots on the

---

[17] Daniel 4:35

bedrock of eternity. To distrust is to spend a lifetime wallowing in doubt, second guesses, and despair.

It turns out that our rare luxury of choice is fraught with uncertainty. It forces us to live in trust or (gulp) by faith. It would be much easier if God eliminated all the uncertainty and just spelled it out for us. He could easily tell us, "Art, not accounting; Phoenix, not Atlanta. Any more questions? Good, now get on with it." Sure, we'd be certain about what to do next, but would life really be any easier or require any less trust? Not hardly.

Check out what happens when God removes all the uncertainty and gives someone the specific details of his game plan: God spoke to Moses from the burning bush. He told him to insult the most powerful ruler on the planet directly to his face. God spoke to Abraham and told him to sacrifice his son as a burnt offering. God instructed Balaam's donkey to speak in fluent Hebrew; then God told Baalam to defy the king of Moab. God knocked the apostle Paul flat on his face with a blinding light and a voice from heaven; then he foretold how Paul must suffer for the sake of God's name. God snapped Elijah to attention by tearing the mountains apart with a great wind, earthquake, and fire; then he told him to return to the people who had killed all the other prophets and sought to hack Elijah to pieces with the sword.

I used to think it would be awesome if God spoke to me through some kind of supernatural sign. But now, after pondering the ramifications, I'm not so sure. If I walk into my office tomorrow morning and God speaks to me from my burning desk, my first thought will be, "Oh no! Please, God; please pick somebody else!" Whatever crazy assignment he is about to give me will require far more trust than I've ever known to be possible in my quivering soul.

Most people in the world don't get the explicit game plan from God, but neither do they bear the weight of uncertainty in their vocational choices. The reason is simple; they have no choice in what they do. God's calling is clear; it's the only available option. This was the experience of Daniel, Shadrach, Meshach, and Abednego.

God did not speak to Daniel from a burning bush, in a bright light, or through a donkey. Daniel and his three buddies didn't read a stack of books on discerning God's calling, attend a seminar, or sit in a cave waiting for a sign or a voice. They didn't sense the call of God while attending an exciting college campus missions conference, and their hearts weren't broken by a particularly eye-catching video of the needy natives in the unreached land of Babylon. Daniel and his buddies were hauled off to Babylon in chains. They had spear points pressed to their backs. God's calling was clear. It was the only available option.

Daniel and his buddies wound up in jobs designed to enhance the prosperity of a pagan king—the corrupt enemy of God's people. The Bible contains no hint of God scrambling around, trying to figure out what went wrong with his perfect plan. Rather, God clearly pronounced, "Thus says the Lord of hosts, the God of Israel, to all the exiles whom I have sent into exile from Jerusalem to Babylon."[18]

"Whom I have sent"—God did it. God put them there. And he put you wherever you are right now. He put me at this writing desk, clicking away on my keyboard. God had just one question for Daniel, Shadrach, Meshach, and Abednego—the same question he has for you and me: "Do you trust me?"

---

[18] Jeremiah 29:4

In the land of opportunity, many people work in marketplace jobs that are a perfect fit for their God-given gifts and interests. Many more are trapped in jobs they hate. Forty-three-year-old accountants get laid off from their accounting jobs and wind up working as tollbooth attendants. They have kids in braces and mortgages to pay. God's calling is clear; it's the only available option. And it feels like exile.

But ponder this—if God is truly God, then your perfect-fit marketplace job or your frustrating exile job is as significant to God as my ministry job. Your vocation is as important to God as the vocation of a pastor, missionary, or evangelist. They are all equally sacred in God's eyes for the simple reason that he alone, the sacred Lord God Almighty, ordains and assigns them all according to his sovereign will. He put us where we are. Some who are in the ministry wave aloft their particular unearned, undeserved sovereign gift of God's grace as if it were a banner of their superior significance over all those who labor in the marketplace. Their smug self-esteem is a raw, horrifying act of pride. It is a mockery of the author and assigner, the giver of our gifts, the Lord God and Master of our divine biographies. "For who makes you different from anyone else? What do you have that you did not receive? And if you did receive it, why do you boast as though you did not?"[19]

God does not look down at any who toil away in marketplace jobs and say to himself, "Well, phooey. How'd that happen? That wasn't part of my plan. I never meant for them to wind up in those frustrating, meaningless jobs. Now let me see, where did I store those alternate backup plans?" He is God. He put you where you

---

[19] 1 Corinthians 4:7 (NIV)

are, and he put me here. In the course of time, the place of his will may change for us—or it may not. That's up to him. Whenever we have the luxury of choice, we must choose wisely, to the best of our limited ability, foresight, and understanding. But all the while, in the uncertainty of those choices (and even in the periodic lack of choices), God has just one question for you and me. It's the question of our eternal destiny: "Do you trust me?"

God is God—infinite and all-powerful. He holds our biographies secure in his hands. He is our mighty captain, and he is worthy of our trust.

CHAPTER 7

WAR IN HIS STORY

No doubt all history in the last resort must be
held by Christians to be a story with a divine plot.

—C. S. Lewis[1]

There is a war going on. All talk of a Christian's
right to live luxuriantly "as a child of the King" in
this atmosphere sounds hollow—especially since
the King himself is stripped for battle.

—John Piper[2]

Stranger, tell the Spartans that we behaved as they
would wish us to, and are buried here.

—Epitaph of three hundred
Spartan warriors[3]

---

[1] C. S. Lewis, *The Discarded Image: An Introduction to Medieval and Renaissance Literature* (New York: Cambridge University Press, 1994), 176.

[2] John Piper, *Desiring God: Meditations of a Christian Hedonist* (Sisters, OR: Multnomah, 1996), 170.

[3] William Golding, "The Hot Gates," *The Sparta Pages,*
http://uts.cc.utexas.edu/~sparta/topics/essays/academic/golding.htm.

*N*o retreat, no surrender. That is Spartan law. And by Spartan law, we will stand and fight and die. A new age has begun. An age of freedom. And all will know that three hundred Spartans gave their last breath to defend it.[4] The year was 480 BC. Leonidas, King of Sparta, and his three hundred men stood side by side, shield to shield in the narrow pass of Thermopylae. Xerxes, King of the Persian Empire, advanced against them with an invading horde of slave warriors, a quarter-million foes, "an army so massive, it shook the ground with its march; so vast, it drank the rivers dry."[5] The ensuing battle cost Leonidas and his men their lives. But their heroic blood inspired the city-states of Greece to unite and crush the Persian menace, thus setting the course for today's free Western world.

Xerxes amassed his slave horde from conquered nations or from nations who willingly bowed before him under threat of annihilation. Among these downtrodden slaves were a people formerly known as the Phoenicians. They were once part of a great civilization and powerful rulers of the Mediterranean. The Phoenician port cites of Tyre and Sidon once ruled the seas, while further inland, a strong network of political alliances secured Phoenicia's regional power. Today, you and I pay tribute to Phoenician culture

---

[4] Ernle Bradford, *Thermopylae: The Battle for the West* (Cambridge, MA: Da Capo Press, 2004); transcript from Zack Snyder, Frank Miller, Kurt Johnstad, Lynn Varley, and Michael Gordon, Screenwriters, *300*, DVD, Directed by Zack Snyder (Warner Home Video, 2007).

[5] Snyder, *300*, (paraphrased).

every time we use our alphabet; it is derived from the ancient Phoenician alphabet.[6]

In about 870 BC, Ethbaal, King of Phoenicia, established a strategic alliance with the kingdom on Phoenicia's eastern border by giving his daughter in marriage to the ruler of those lands. The Phoenician princess joined her new husband in the hilltop city of Samaria, where she eventually became one of the most powerful and most notorious queens in Mediterranean history. Her future dynasty seemed destined to rule Samaria and its surrounding lands, effectively incorporating them into the greater Phoenician empire. But her reign was weakened when her husband died in a relatively unimportant, distant battle. In the resulting power vacuum, she and her male heirs were slaughtered by her political enemies, who had long sought to rid their homeland of her imported Phoenician culture and religion.

The city of Samaria, along with its surrounding lands, remained independent of Phoenicia; thus it was able to protect its unique religious heritage and cultural identity. In the centuries that followed, the entire Phoenician Empire slid into decline and eventually fell to the Persians. Hence, a once proud and mighty Phoenician civilization ended up groveling at the feet of Xerxes, enslaved. Its citizens became human fodder, forced to charge the spears of Leonidas and his three hundred Spartans in the narrow pass of Thermopylae. So who was this Phoenician princess, anyway? And what's the big deal with the hilltop city of Samaria?

Her name was Jezebel. And in those years, Samaria was the capital city of Israel. Jezebel and her Jewish husband, King Ahab, were the infamous Baal-worshiping monarchs of Israel. Her chief

---

6 Steven Rogers Fischer, *A History of Writing* (London: Reaktion Books, 2003), 90.

political enemy was the prophet Elijah—the very same guy who stood on a mountain and heard the voice of God. That game plan God spelled out for Elijah in explicit detail was the political mop-up plan that would rid Israel of Jezebel's Phoenician, Baal-worshiping religion.

Hidden at the center of these events is the most intriguing detail of all—the death of King Ahab. The whole saga turned on that event. If Ahab had lived, then Jezebel would have remained in power, and Israel would have become a radically different nation—likely a province of Phoenicia. But God had a different plan. The Bible records a full account of King Ahab's death. He disguised himself for battle, like a common soldier, to avoid being singled out for attack. (What an inspiring leader.) Rather than a glorious, hand-to-hand dual with an opposing champion, Ahab died as follows: "A certain man drew his bow at random and struck the king of Israel between the scale armor and the breastplate."[7]

That's it. Ahab died. There was only a small gap in his armor, but some unnamed, rank and file, grunt soldier randomly twanged an arrow in the general direction of Israel's army . . . and turned the epic tide of world history.

This common soldier probably had no idea where his arrow landed. He certainly didn't know he had killed the disguised king. As the years passed, he undoubtedly grew too old for the grinding toil of ancient soldiery. He probably trudged back home to his peasant village and lived out his days in total obscurity. He went to his grave, clueless of the fact that God used him to depose Israel's

---

[7] 1 Kings 22:34

corrupt monarchy—that he shaped the course of history. He did his duty and then went home. That's it.

When you and I watch war movies, we imagine ourselves as the fearless leader at the front of the charge—the star of the movie and the hero of the war. It's amazing how the hero can run clear across the battlefield and sustain only minor injuries while everyone around him is blown to bits, special-effects body parts flying in all directions. None of us ever imagine ourselves as the person who starts the charge nine rows back, third from the left—the one who gets blown to bits in the first volley. This is the magic of Hollywood. All of us get to feel like the hero, the one who makes it—or at least dies in a glorious feat of triumph—the one who is significant. Well, I have some disappointing news: life ain't a Hollywood movie.

As it turns out, God placed most of us nine rows back, third from the left—or better yet, nine pews back, third from the left. We imagine that people in full-time Christian ministry are the real heroes—the people who are truly significant in the epic of eternity. They're out in front, in the pulpit, or on the front lines of the mission field. Meanwhile, we're in back, installing hardwood floors, writing legal briefs, designing hydraulic hose fittings, and cooking orders to go—just unnamed, rank and file, grunt soldiers. We're destined to be blown to bits while the superstars get the glory and do something significant for God.

But God Almighty doesn't need superstar Christians to fight his battles for him. Instead, he does the unimaginable: he takes up our ordinary, everyday lives, and he guides them through time like a random arrow. He turns the epic tide of eternity with them. We live our days in total obscurity, clueless that God is using us to shape his epic masterpiece. We do our duty and then go home.

That's it. But when we get there, we will look into the eyes of our mighty captain, and then all will become clear. We will finally see that our lives mattered. They mattered to God.

RANDOM-ARROW LIVES

God didn't call us to heaven—yet. He called us to war. The Bible says, "The night is far gone; the day is at hand. So then let us cast off the works of darkness and put on the armor of light."[8] The armor of light, not the Snuggie of light. We are at war, because God is at war, and he calls us to follow him into the heart of it.

I have friends who feel God couldn't possibly be engaged in mortal combat. To them, the very idea that God is at war demeans his sovereignty. They point out the fact that God could annihilate his enemies with a single word. He even has angels who are powerful enough to defeat Satan and throw him into the bottomless pit. So God obviously isn't fighting some epic battle of eternity; he'd win the battle instantly. This objection to a warring God is well-reasoned; the logic is superb. There's just one problem: from cover to cover, the Bible says God is at war, and so are we.

It boggles my mind, but God, in his perfect wisdom, decided that his name is most glorified by waging an epic battle of good against evil, light against darkness. St. Augustine said, "God judged it better to bring good out of evil than to suffer no evil to exist."[9] And then God sovereignly decided that you and I should

---

[8] Romans 13:12

[9] Augustine, quoted in Charles G. Herbermann, ed., et al, *The Catholic Encyclopedia: An International Work of Reference on the Constitution, Doctrine, Discipline, and History of the Catholic Church, Vol. 5.* (New York: Robert Appleton, 1909), 651.

live in a world plagued by this evil. We live in a fallen world—a world at war.

Have you ever noticed how the heroes of our favorite movies are essentially selfless? They see beyond themselves. They fight against evil, selflessly rescue the weak, serve others, and give hope to the hopeless. They see a bigger story—something beyond their own little lives. Consequently, their own little story takes on epic significance. Villains, however, are typically selfish jerks. They see nothing beyond themselves. They selfishly consume everyone in their path and use others to fuel the story of their own little, self-centered lives. And we loathe them for it.

Hollywood discovered this formula long ago. We love to watch selfless heroes on the big screen. (This is remarkable, given that we are one of the most high-consuming, self-centered societies of all time.) Hollywood can crank out a box office hit by simply thrusting a selfless hero into the middle of an epic conflict between good and evil. We'll pay big bucks to sit in a theater and be swept up into a story bigger than ourselves. For two hours, something deep inside of us yearns for the story to be more than just high-definition make-believe. We long for our own little lives to be part of the epic. It's our old ache for eternal significance—our God-given longing to be part of his story. It turns out, we *are* part of the story. We're right in the middle of it.

Eternity is God's story. Within that story, he authored a time of war. There couldn't possibly be any greater epic. This story, the one that sweeps up our lives and gives them eternal significance, is the story of the Bible. Humans enter the scene on the first page of the Bible. We had no part in eternity past—the time before Genesis 1:1—but then God created us and swept us up into the rest of his story. This is stunning. Our own little stories (our lives) have a beginning, but they have no ending. God says we will "reign forever and ever."[10] To see our place in God's great epic, we need only look at the Bible.

In the first age of humankind, God created our ancestors, Adam and Eve. Then God installed them as the rightful king and queen over all the earth. "Let them have dominion . . . over all the earth."[11] They were his royal regents—stewards at the bequest of God, their great emperor and the Lord of the universe. Then the deceiver, Satan, found humankind's weakness—pride. Through it, he deposed the rightful king and queen of the earth and usurped the throne. Humankind fell, and with it, all the earth fell under a curse—the rule of Satan, "the prince of the power of the air"[12] and "the ruler of this world."[13] In that instant, humankind was swept up into a war to defeat Satan and regain the throne of the earth.

You and I are the sons and daughters of Adam and Eve. We are the rightful heirs to the throne of the earth, "heirs—heirs of God and fellow heirs with Christ."[14] As such, we are called into the heart of the battle. Our mighty captain, Jesus Christ, came to earth and made the ultimate selfless sacrifice: he suffered the penalty for our treasonous pride and thereby dealt Satan a mortal wound. But Satan still lives. He roams the earth, "seeking someone to devour."[15] God, in his wisdom, granted Satan a window of time—a time of war.

However, at the appointed hour, Jesus Christ will return to earth, fiercely arrayed for battle. He will destroy Satan and all who

---

[10] Revelation 22:5
[11] Genesis 1:26
[12] Ephesians 2:2
[13] John 12:31
[14] Romans 8:17
[15] 1 Peter 5:8

stand with him. God will redeem the earth and set it free from the curse. "The creation itself will be set free from its bondage to corruption and obtain the freedom of the glory of the children of God."[16] Then God will once again install us as his royal regents, kings and queens of the earth—stewards at the bequest of our great emperor. "You have made them a kingdom and priests to our God, and they shall reign on the earth."[17] The time of war will be over forever.

Wow. That's quite a story. It's big, grand, heroic, and everything else that makes a story great. But it seems totally irrelevant to the daily grind of our lives. Somehow, all those epic images get lost in the piles of laundry, the 8:30 a.m. production meetings, and the past-due budget reports. Not much in my life feels very epic. I've chalked up some epic failures, but nothing epic in the war-against-evil sense. And that part about being kings and queens of the earth—most of the time, I'd be happy just to be king of my recliner.

Long ago, there was an unnamed, rank and file, grunt soldier who randomly twanged an arrow in the general direction of Israel's army. He probably felt exactly the same way about his life. *Epic? Yeah, right.*

The call to follow Christ isn't meant to give us nice, comfortable, prosperous lives. It's meant to give us battle-scarred lives, just like our mighty captain's life. He bears the unspeakable scars of the cross. God calls us into war and assigns us a crucial role to fill in

---

[16] Romans 8:21
[17] Revelation 5:10

his epic of eternity. We may stand nine rows back, third from the left, clutching a few bent arrows and a worn-out bow, but God turns the epic tide of eternity with our little, random-arrow lives.

God assigned us a time on earth between the cross of Christ (the mortal wounding of Satan) and Christ's future victorious return. It's like the months between D-Day and VE-Day during World War II. D-Day was the turning point of the war in Europe. The Allied forces landed on the beaches of Normandy and delivered a mortal wound to Hitler's Nazi tyranny. The events of that day essentially assured the Allies' victory in Europe. But ultimate victory, VE-Day, required eleven more months of grueling, bloody warfare. In all, more than 180,000 rank and file Allied soldiers were killed in action on European soil during those eleven months.[18]

Every year during Christmas week, we get caught up in tranquil images of a manger scene, baby Jesus, some sheep, a few shepherds, and maybe a gentle ox over in the corner. But in the raging battle of eternity, the birth of Jesus was the offensive strike that set the stage for D-Day—the blow that crushed the serpent's head under the cosmic weight of a blood-soaked cross. Victory! The cross of Christ is D-Day. His return is VE-Day. You and I are assigned crucial roles in the grueling battle that lies between those days. We will get scars, but those scars will make us more like Jesus Christ, our captain.

The epic battle of eternity is not only fought "out there" somewhere by legions of warring angels in the heavenly realm; it is also fought in the everyday context of software installations, diesel engine repairs, southern-style barbecue, and shopping trips to Walmart. God chooses to fight this epic battle, in part, through

[18] Charles B. MacDonald and Martin Blumenson, "Defeat of Germany," *A Concise History of World War II,* ed. Vincent J. Esposito (New York: Frederick A. Praeger, 1964), 125.

the regular toil of our lives. The Battle of the Bulge was one of the most important battles fought in the months between D-Day and VE-Day. Philip Yancey writes:

> The soldiers recalled how they spent a particular day. One sat in a foxhole all day; once or twice, a German tank drove by, and he shot at it. Others played cards and frittered away the time. A few got involved in furious firefights. Mostly, the day passed like any other day for an infantryman on the front. Later, they learned they had just participated in one of the largest, most decisive engagements of the war, the Battle of the Bulge. It did not *feel* decisive to any of them at the time, because none had the big picture of what was happening elsewhere.
>
> Great victories are won when ordinary people execute their assigned tasks, and a faithful person does not debate each day whether he or she is in the mood to follow the sergeant's orders or go to work at a boring job. We exercise faith by responding to the task that lies before us.[19]

Our task is to do our God-given duty nine rows back, third from the left. We are to be bulldozer operators, engineers, florists, and real estate agents who live and work with the goal of making God look supremely valuable in our lives. We fulfill that duty in the context of our regular, everyday work. We drive, design, ar-

---

[19] Philip Yancey, "Living with Furious Opposites," *Christianity Today*, September 4, 2000, www.christianitytoday.com/ct/2000/september4/4.70.html.

range, and sell with hearts determined to glorify our great emperor in the task he sets before us. In so doing, we fill the world—every nook and cranny of it—with God's glorious name.

We totally misunderstand our place in the battle if we merely hunker down in church and nervously wait for the return of our captain. That's the old sacred-secular divide at work again, telling us to hang out on the sacred side of the divide; it's safe over there. Our battle assignment isn't to spend as much time as possible hiding in the bunker of cradle-to-grave church programs. It is, rather, to venture out and fight Satan by filling the earth with God's glory so the dozer cab, office, flower shop, and open house are all occupied by someone reflecting the name and values of Jesus Christ.

World War II Allied Commander General Douglas MacArthur left the Philippines (Bataan) as the invading Japanese swarmed in and overtook the islands. Darrow Miller, author of the book *Life-Work*, writes:

> MacArthur sent word back to the Philippine resistance: "I came out of Bataan and *I shall return.*". . .
> He wanted the Philippine resistance to continue to fight because he would be coming back to the Philippines. Two years and seven months after his message was sent to the world, he returned to the Philippines to restore its freedom.
>
> This is essentially what Christ has called his people to do. He conquered death at the resurrection; he has gone to the Father. . . . In the meantime, he tells his people, "Fight on, for I shall return!"[20]

---

[20] D. L. Miller, *LifeWork*, 323.

God made Jesus Christ head of the church, "which is his body, the fullness of him who fills all in all."[21] The church (all who trust in Christ) is the body of Christ. Through that body, Christ fills all in all. This is mind-blowing. Through us, God chooses to fill the entire universe with his lordship, wisdom, and fathomless glory. He guides our random-arrow lives into the spheres of our vocations—our work, roles, and relationships—our little sliver of the all in all. He doesn't ask us to conquer the world single-handedly on his behalf. He says, rather, "Whatever you do, do all to the glory of God."[22]

When we look beyond ourselves, we begin to see a bigger story, something beyond the stories of our own little lives. We glimpse our place in God's great masterpiece of eternity, and suddenly, our lives take on epic significance. Our mighty captain made the ultimate selfless sacrifice. He bears the unspeakable scars of war. And now, his call to us is clear: "Come, follow me."

FOR SUCH A TIME AS THIS

While Xerxes drove his horde against the shields and spears of three hundred Spartans, his wife, Queen of the Persian Empire, remained in Susa, the Persian capital. Her name was Esther. The Bible devotes an entire book to her story.[23]

From orphaned Jewish girl to imperial queen, Esther's rise to power is a remarkable story in itself.[24] But we remember her best

---

[21] Ephesians 1:22–23

[22] 1 Corinthians 10:31

[23] English Bibles traditionally translate the name Xerxes as Ahasuerus (a name equivalent to Xerxes), e.g., Esther 1:1.

[24] Some historians believe she was queen to Artaxerxes II, great-grandson of Xerxes. Either way, she was queen of the Persian Empire.

as the woman who challenged a king and saved the Jewish race from annihilation. Her entire life was an arching arrow, perfectly aimed at a single, crucial moment in history. She was born, orphaned, and swept up into royalty "for such a time as this."[25] Those words, from the book of Esther, wave like a banner over her life. Today, most of us quietly long for those words to be the story of our lives, too.

We dream of our grand adventure, our epic moment in history, our very own "for such a time as this." But then the alarm goes off. It's Monday morning, and the reality of what faces us doesn't even come close to the excitement of Esther's story. Few of us will make headline news; fewer still will visibly change the course of world history. Esther's life was remarkable and inspiring, but let's be honest: it's impossible for most of us to relate to. Not only was she the Queen of the Persian Empire, but God also obviously guided her life so she could impact an important event in world history. By comparison, our mundane moments feel ridiculously insignificant.

It seems like we're just killing time between God's D-Day and his VE-Day. Those turbulent days in biblical history were obviously important to God's grand epic of eternity. And it's clear that the last days—the end times when Jesus Christ comes back to put an end to this war—will also be critical to God's epic story. But today, this in-between age is boring. It seems as if God somehow drifted off to sleep and lost track of time—our particular moment in time. Most of us will toil our days away in marketplace jobs, a few of us in ministry jobs, and then we'll go home. That's it.

---

[25] Esther 4:14

But God is still God. He is no less God today than he was in Esther's day. And he is no less God today than he will be in the end times. "I the Lord do not change."[26] For all of eternity—past, present, and future—God is God, infinite and all-powerful, "the same yesterday and today and forever."[27]

The truth of God's unchanging nature illumines a stunning implication for our regular, everyday, mundane moment in time. We can see it even more clearly by the light of two additional statements from the Bible: God "works all things according to the counsel of his will,"[28] and he "upholds the universe by the word of his power."[29] So, we have an unchanging God who actively upholds the universe and works all things according to his will, and he does all of this right now, at this very instant—this regular, everyday, mundane moment in time.

Your life ripples with the intense providence of God—the same God who guided Esther's life, the same God who currently upholds your body and 200 billion galaxies, and who will one day bring to pass the cataclysmic events of the end times. This God, the sovereign God of the universe, did not drift off to sleep and lose track of your life. He is, instead, actively shaping your moment in time. It is his perfect, good, unfathomable, intentional creation, and it shapes the future course of eternity.

God designed and orchestrated the epic chapter of eternity past, the entire cosmos, and all of human history with the intent of placing you and me in our unique vocations—the exact places where we work and live—right now. Then he carries this instant (our place in the epic) forward as an indispensable element in his

---

[26] Malachi 3:6
[27] Hebrews 13:8
[28] Ephesians 1:11
[29] Hebrews 1:3

ongoing masterpiece of eternity. This instant—this Tuesday afternoon at 2:32 during which I type these words and the instant in which you read them—is infused with the infinite. It is infused with God.

There are no insignificant moments in time. There's no such thing, for God is the author of time. If he were merely a human author, then you and I could review his work each day and give it a rating: "That stuff he wrote back in Esther's day—wow, that was top-notch work, worthy of five stars. But lately, he's been off his game; the stuff he's writing now seems mundane and trifling. Two stars at best." God, however, is God. His authorship is always perfect. When you and I slip into despair and begin to doubt the significance of our particular moment in time, we are in essence giving God's wisdom a two-star rating. But the perfection of God's wisdom does not ebb and flow over time, and neither does his infinite glory.

The terms *infinite* and *perfect* are not relative terms; they are absolute terms. There's no such thing as *more* infinite or *more* perfect. Hence, if his authorship of our moment in time is perfect, then there is no other moment in time, past or future, that is more perfect or significant—not Esther's "for such a time as this" and not the moment when "the trumpet will sound, and the dead will be raised imperishable."[30] Whoa, it feels presumptuous to claim that this unremarkable moment on a Tuesday afternoon is as significant as Esther's moment in history and the moment of the resurrection. And the claim *is* presumptuous if the significance of this moment depends on you and me—but it doesn't.

---

[30] 1 Corinthians 15:52

The significance of this moment in time rests solely in the author of this moment in time. The significance of Esther's moment was not derived from Esther or her brave actions but from God. His glory and significance are infinite. He owns it all. He is the source of it all. Consequently, the significance of this moment is derived solely from him.

Perhaps an illustration will help. Today, the significance of a Van Gogh painting is not derived from the painting itself but from the fact that Van Gogh painted it. If you discover a formerly unknown Van Gogh painting in your attic, then you no longer need to worry about paying for your kid's braces. An original Van Gogh would be worth millions of dollars, sight unseen. At first glance, your discovery might appear to be an insignificant, mundane, boring old painting. But if it's a Van Gogh, its astonishing value is derived solely from the significance of the artist. This illustration is imperfect in many ways, of course. But it gives us a faint image of the truth. God infuses each moment with himself. There can be no greater significance—our everyday moments in time have astonishing value.

Today we can't see the whole story; we can barely see a tiny glimpse of it. We won't see the rest of the story until we see the author face to face. "For now we see through a glass, darkly; but then face to face: now I know in part; but then shall I know even as also I am known."[31]

You and I see extraordinary moments in time, like Esther's, and assign great importance to them. But we have a hard time seeing the eternal value of our plain, ordinary moments. That's okay—we're humans, not God. Even within the context of our

---

[31] 1 Corinthians 12:13 (KJV)

everyday lives, there are certain moments that feel vastly more significant than others. During a business lunch meeting, I once swallowed a heaping spoonful of straight-up, flesh-incinerating wasabi hot paste. (I mistook it for guacamole.) As I opened my mouth, the dumbfounded look of horror on everyone else's faces should have warned me—my personality was about to be permanently altered. That moment when the wasabi hit my tongue is more significant to me than any moment in any lunch meeting before or since. And that's okay. I'll see the significance of all those other forgotten lunch meetings when I see the author face to face.

God is the author of your moment in time. He's the author of mine, too. In our eyes, our moments may look mundane and ridiculously insignificant, but in God's eyes, they are eternally significant. We don't need to conjure up our significance by impressing God with the amazing stuff we can do for him. Instead, we need to be faithful to the task he sets before us. "Whatever your hand finds to do, do it with all your might,"[32] wrote the author of Ecclesiastes. That task is our vocation—our work, roles, and relationships. God sets our task before us right now, in this moment. This is our place in the epic battle of eternity. This is our very own, God-authored "for such a time as this."

WHERE THE BATTLE RAGES

We are at war—a war so fierce that Jesus Christ split the epic of eternity with his blood-soaked cry, "'Eli, Eli, lema sabachthani?' that is, 'My God, my God, why have you forsaken me?'"[33] In wag-

---

[32] Ecclesiastes 9:10 (NIV)
[33] Matthew 27:46

ing war against Satan, God sent his perfect Son, our champion, to suffer and die on a Roman cross. If we follow him into the heart of battle, then we shouldn't be surprised when our lives and vocations—our God-authored places to stand and fight—sometimes feel a tiny little bit like a cross. We read Foxe's book of martyrs, and we marvel. But then we whine and complain about the drudgery and insignificance of our work—our obscure "for such a time as this." Our labor seems frustrating, futile, hard, not particularly suited to our gifts, and some of our coworkers are vulgar jerks. "Then Jesus told his disciples, 'If anyone would come after me, let him deny himself and take up his cross and follow me. For whoever would save his life will lose it, but whoever loses his life for my sake will find it.'"[34]

We're called to take up our cross and follow Jesus *into* the daily grind of life, not out of it. The battle rages in our offices, job sites, kitchens, and truck cabs. There, in some way, we reflect God's glory and bear his name, nine rows back, third from the left. George MacLeod wrote:

> Jesus was not crucified in a cathedral between two candles, but on a cross between two thieves; on the town garbage-heap; at a crossroad so cosmopolitan that they had to write his title in Hebrew and in Latin and in Greek . . . at the kind of place where cynics talk smut, and thieves curse, and soldiers gamble. Because that is where he died. And that is what he died about. And that is where

---

[34] Matthew 16:24–25

churchmen should be and what churchmanship should be about.[35]

A wave of confusion has swept through our churches. We've linked suffering for Jesus solely to Christian ministry. We've totally disconnected our everyday toil from taking up our cross and following our mighty captain into battle. But we are mistaken; the battle rages all around us. We're not off duty when we're at work. The epic battle of eternity is not fought solely in the context of official Christian ministry. It rages directly in front of us in the regular, everyday tasks before us.

When we were young newlyweds, Misty finished her master's degree and landed her first teaching job—ninth-grade English in a rough, drug-ridden public school on the wrong side of the tracks. A few of our older friends who worked in full-time Christian ministry were deeply disappointed by Misty's willingness to even consider working at a public school. Our friends strongly believed the battle is fought in full-time ministry, not in so-called secular work. To them, that meant Misty should teach in a private Christian school, not a public (secular) school. They meant well, and they genuinely wanted us to serve the Lord, but they held a profound misunderstanding of where the battle is fought. One of them came over to our apartment and shared this concern: "By teaching in a public school, you are wasting your gifts."

Misty and I still had much to learn about life, ministry, and faith, and we didn't want to question the wisdom of a mature Christian friend. But we couldn't help wondering, *So, teaching in a Christian school, where the kids mostly come from supportive homes, is*

---

[35] George MacLeod, *Only One Way Left* (Glasgow: Wild Goose Publications, 1956), 38.

doing something for God; but teaching in a rough school, where many of the kids come from homes shattered by drugs and crime, is wasting Misty's gifts? Um, there seems to be a problem with this picture. For the next three years, Misty taught in that public school.

I've lost count of how many times I've heard missionaries and church leaders say, "Satan fights hardest against people who are in full-time ministry, because they're the ones on the front lines of the battle. Satan isn't worried about people in secular jobs, because secular jobs take Christians out of the battle." *Um, there seems to be a problem with this picture.* You and I need to be gracious to people who say this, but we also need to hold up the truth. Martin Luther passionately held up the truth. He insisted the battle is fought in the context of everyday marketplace life; that's where we take up our cross and suffer.

> I ask where our suffering is to be found. I shall soon tell you: Run through all the stations of life, from the lowest to the highest, and you will find what you are looking for. . . . Therefore do not worry where you can find suffering. That is not necessary. Simply live as an earnest Christian . . . and fulfill your office faithfully and loyally. Let the devil worry where he can find a piece of wood out of which to make a cross for you, and the world where it can find a branch out of which to make a scourge for your hide.[36]

---

[36] Luther, quoted in Gustaf Wingren, *Luther on Vocation*, trans. Carl C. Rasmussen (Eugene, OR: Wipf and Stock, 2004), 29–30.

In the Old Testament, we read about a guy named Job who suffered horrific pain and loss under direct satanic attack. Job was not a prophet, preacher, priest, or missionary. He was, rather, an extremely successful businessman. The Bible says that Job, the businessman, was "blameless and upright, one who feared God."[37] In Hebrews 11, we read about sixteen heroes of the faith in "the hall of faith." Of the sixteen, only one was in a line of work we would consider "the ministry." The rest were businesspeople, government officials, or military leaders—except for Samson, the playboy, and Rahab, the former prostitute. Most martyrs are everyday people simply living as earnest Christians, steadfastly fulfilling their marketplace vocations. They are not professional ministers.

The confusion is devastating and haunting. I've seen the following scenario happen over and over—a Christian hates his marketplace job. It's frustrating, futile, hard, not particularly suited to his gifts, and some of his coworkers are vulgar jerks. So he sets out to find a more significant job in missions, where he can do something meaningful for God. He's ready and willing to suffer for Jesus in the jungles of the mission field but not in the jungles of the corporate economy. It would appear that as far as he's concerned, his former coworkers can all go to hell. He holds to a profound misunderstanding of where the battle is fought.

To Martin Luther, who was himself a pastor, a call to full-time Christian ministry, motivated by our irksome jobs or a desire to do something more meaningful for God, would be nothing less than a "satanic perversion."[38] There is, however, a good and legitimate call to ministry.

---

[37] Job 1:1
[38] Wingren, *Luther on Vocation*, 90.

If you have a knack for teaching, a passion for studying the Bible, a love for helping people when they're at their worst, and those who know you best keep saying, "You know, you really ought to consider being a pastor," then for crying out loud, get to seminary! If you are burdened for a lost tribe in the jungles of South America and you have the ability to carry the gospel to that tribe, then get on an airplane and get on with it! Do it with all your might! But if you sense a vague, general call into ministry because you want to make your life count for eternity rather than waste it in secular work, then you need to pause and gaze upon the cross of Jesus Christ.

We are each called to fill our unique spheres in the world with God's glorious name. The battle rages everywhere—it rages in the heart of every single human being. For most of us, taking up our cross and following him means a lifetime of steadfastly laboring as mechanics, accounts payable clerks, systems analysts, and homemakers. It's a full-time call, not a part-time call or a 5 or 10 percent call. We may be able to volunteer 36 hours each month at a church outreach ministry, but compare those 36 hours to the 160 hours we spend with our coworkers each month or the 530 hours we spend in all the other spheres of life. We are not spectators, sitting on the outside looking in at lives that count for eternity. We are, rather, smack in the middle of it. We're at war. Today is battle day, not Snuggie day.

CHAPTER 8

CREATED TO CREATE

In the beginning, God created . . .

—Genesis 1:1

Then God said, "Let us make man in our image, after our likeness."

—Genesis 1:26

The Lord God took the man and put him in the garden of Eden to work it and keep it.

—Genesis 2:15

What's the point of being you? There's only one right answer. If you and I get it wrong, life feels like a bewildering exercise in hopeless futility. But if we get it right, life—even with its thistles and thorns—radiates with unimaginable joy.

The answer is in the Bible. The point of being you—the one and only, unique person standing in your distinct matrix of circumstances, relationships, and vocation—is to reflect the glory of God. "Man's chief end is to glorify God, and to enjoy him forever."[1] That's why he made you. That's the whole point of your being you. Three times in the first chapter of Ephesians, we read that God created us and called us to himself "to the praise of his glory."[2] In the book of Isaiah, God says, "Bring my sons from afar and my daughters from the end of the earth, everyone who is called by my name, whom I created for my glory."[3] God created us and everything else in the universe for his glory. It's all about him—not you or me. "For by him all things were created, in heaven and on earth, visible and invisible, whether thrones or dominions or rulers or authorities—all things were created through

---

[1] This is the first statement and foundational precept of the *Westminster Shorter Catechism*. See Orthodox Presbyterian Church, *The Westminster Confession of Faith and Catechisms: with Proof Texts* (Lawrenceville, GA: The Christian Education and Publications Committee of the Presbyterian Church in America, 2005), 355.

[2] Ephesians 1:6, 12, 14

[3] Isaiah 43:6–7

him and for him."[4] "Worthy are you, our Lord and God, to receive glory and honor and power, for you created all things, and by your will they existed and were created."[5]

In some unfathomable way, God created you and me like one-of-a-kind facets of an infinite diamond. We are uniquely shaped to reflect a particular aspect of his glory. This is mind-blowing: the shape of you somehow reflects a unique facet of God, the diamond of the universe—a facet that only you, and forever only you, can reflect. God aims to display his glory throughout all the universe. Our job is to reflect our one-of-a-kind facet of his diamond glory in every moment and sphere of our lives. Our unceasing prayer should be, "Oh, Lord, shape me and hone me to be a perfect reflection of You, the unique reflection that You made me to be." St. Thomas Acquinas once said, "It would take an infinite number of human beings to mirror back the infinite facets of the Godhead. Each person reflects only a small—but beautiful—part of the whole."[6]

I gaze out our kitchen window in the quiet, cold nights of the subarctic winter, and I behold a breathtaking sight—the aurora borealis (northern lights) dancing high above the majestic peaks of the Wrangell mountains. The aurora phenomenon occurs when trillions of electrically charged particles, which are flung from the surface of the sun, hurl through space and collide with atoms in the earth's upper atmosphere. This collision ignites the visible discharge of energy I see as an aurora display of solar glory. Each tiny particle displays its unique glimmer of the sun's magnificence. Each particle stands in its one-of-a-kind matrix of space and time.

---

[4] Colossians 1:16
[5] Revelation 4:11
[6] Acquinas, quoted in Michael Novak, *Business as a Calling: Work and the Examined Life* (New York: Free Press, 1996), 34.

Of course, compared to the blazing, twenty-four million degree temperature of the sun itself, the aurora particles are "accounted as nothing."[7] Yet in this hour of bitter cold and darkness, they are "the light of the world."[8]

The glory of an aurora particle is not its own glory. It is the sun's glory. The glory you and I each reflect is not our own. It is God's. But in no way does this diminish the significance of our lives or vocations (our place in the dazzling display). Instead, it gives us unfathomable significance: God bestows to us the significance of his infinitely glorious Son. There can be no greater significance in all eternity. I don't gaze into the winter sky and think to myself, *Well, just look at all those pathetic little insignificant particles up there; they're totally meaningless in the grand scheme of things.* No way. In the wonder and amazement of the moment, the only thought going through my awestruck mind is, *Wow!*

There is, however, one critical distinction between our lives and the life of an aurora particle. A particle flares off its reflection of solar glory in just a tiny fraction of a second. You and I are everlasting. Our stories have a beginning but no ending. We will uniquely reflect God's glory forever. You have a unique vocation to fulfill right now—roles to fill, relationships to maintain, and tasks to do. We wake up to this reality every Monday morning. Most of us, though, never stop to ponder the fact that we will also have a vocation in heaven—a unique place and role to reflect God's glory for all eternity. Remarkably, God uses today's vocations, complete with their thistles and thorns, to uniquely shape, hone, and forge each of us into everlasting reflections of his glory.

---

[7] Daniel 4:35
[8] Matthew 5:14

But I'm jumping ahead to heaven and spoiling the end of this book, so I'll temporarily leave the topic of heaven with this quote from C. S. Lewis. Then we'll get back to the stark reality of our fallen planet earth.

> Your soul has a curious shape because it is a hollow made to fit a particular swelling in the infinite contours of the Divine substance, or a key to unlock one of the doors in the house with many mansions. For it is not humanity in the abstract that is to be saved, but you—you the individual reader. . . . Your place in heaven will seem to be made for you and you alone, because you were made for it—made for it stitch by stitch as a glove is made for a hand.[9]

You, the individual reader, are made in the image of God right now. Your morning experience may be different from mine, but when I stagger out of bed each morning and look in the mirror, "the image of God" is not the first thing that comes to mind. (I'm fairly certain it's not Misty's first impression of me, either.) Yet God clearly says the bedraggled face in the mirror is made in his image: "God created man in his own image, in the image of God he created him; male and female he created them."[10]

How is this possible? God's original purpose for humankind was (and still is) that they should be *image-bearers*—his image and glory reflected in us. But how exactly are we supposed to reflect the image of God? We find our answer in the first job description

---

[9] C. S. Lewis, *The Problem of Pain* (San Francisco: HarperCollins, 2001), 152.
[10] Genesis 1:27

given to humans: "'Let them have dominion over the fish of the sea and over the birds of the heavens and over the livestock and over all the earth.' . . . And God blessed them. And God said to them, 'Be fruitful and multiply and fill the earth and subdue it.'"[11]

The answer, in part, is work. We bear the image of God by working. Our dominion of the earth reflects the image of our great emperor, who reigns with ultimate dominion. When we work, we imitate God. We fill the earth with his image. The work we're talking about here—having dominion, filling, subduing—is regular, everyday, marketplace work: we manage the resources, tend the cattle, harvest the crops, grow societies, create cultures, and flourish. "What is man that you are mindful of him, and the son of man that you care for him? Yet you have made him a little lower than the heavenly beings and crowned him with glory and honor. You have given him dominion over the works of your hands; you have put all things under his feet."[12]

God hard-wired us to organize, build, and manage. He created us to create. Then God included our work—work that reflects him as Lord, Creator, Sustainer, and Redeemer—in his pronouncement, "And behold, it was very good." Our work, therefore, is not a curse. It is, rather, a blessing. It is intricately wrapped up into the very essence and purpose of humankind. God made you and me to reflect his glory. A primary means by which we fulfill that purpose is through our work. For some of us, that work may be a full-time ministry position. For most of us, though, that work will be a full-time marketplace job. Either way, the sovereign pronouncement echoes, "And behold, it was very good."

---

[11] Genesis 1:26, 28
[12] Psalm 8:4–6

WE ARE GOD'S EARTH-SHAPERS

We don't organize, build, manage, and create merely in the abstract—in an imaginary realm where the product of our labor is devoid of tangible reality, a worshipful charade of sorts. We work, rather, with real things and real people in real space and time. Consequently, real stuff gets done; real things are created. Our work shapes societies and cultures, the earth, and human lives. In God's inscrutable wisdom, not only does he forge eternity with our random-arrow lives, but he also uses our lives to forge the shape of the present. The world is different right now because you did whatever you did today. Expense reports, sales contracts, praying with a friend, vacuuming a floor, or installing a granite countertop—all these tasks shape the present. All of them leave fingerprints on eternity. All of them rely on the sustaining hand of God.

We are God's earth-shapers. He could have created the earth in a completely finished state—a few billion perfect people who live in a thriving, God-centered society and tend an exquisitely balanced, flourishing global ecology. But he didn't. He plunked down just two people and said, "Be fruitful and multiply and fill the earth and subdue it."[13] His aim is to be glorified not only in the reflection of his human-imaged glory, but also in his ongoing transformation of the earth through our work. God told us to shape the earth. His mandate was not, "Keep things the way they are," and it has never been, "Return things to the way they were."

---

[13] Genesis 1:28

Eden was just the starting line. People longing for a return to Eden desire the wrong end of the journey. They need to look in the other direction. The finish line will blow our minds. Unbelievably, God designed it with our fingerprints all over it.

God issued the mandate to work *before* the fall of humankind. It was the very first thing he said to us. And the mandate didn't change after the fall; it just got a lot harder. Now most of our work is rework—repairing, correcting, protecting, sweating, aching, and pulling weeds, thorns, and thistles. It's exasperating. Yet through it all, God shapes us and the world for his glory. God's sustaining hand works through us and upholds our feeble efforts. "He is before all things, and in him all things hold together."[14] "He upholds the universe by the word of his power."[15] "In his hand is the life of every living thing and the breath of all mankind."[16]

You are everlasting. The fall of humankind and the resulting curse are temporary—a time of war, an hour of bitter cold and darkness. But the Son will soon return. "On his robe and on his thigh he has a name written, King of kings and Lord of lords."[17] Day will break, the war will be over, and the curse will be lifted. We will flourish in our vocations. And the point of it all—the point of you—will remain unchanged throughout all eternity. "Whoever serves, as one who serves by the strength that God supplies—in order that in everything God may be glorified through Jesus Christ. To him belong glory and dominion forever and ever. Amen."[18]

---

[14] Colossians 1:17
[15] Hebrews 1:3
[16] Job 12:10
[17] Revelation 19:16
[18] 1 Peter 4:11

WORK AS WORSHIP

They're dead broke, financially. But in terms of job satisfaction, they're some of the wealthiest people on the planet: artists, *true* artists—starving artists.

Most people want to separate work as far as possible from the rest of life, thinking, *It's just a way to pay the bills.* They cage work in the eight-to-five window, and then they think about it as little as possible. *Why ruin Saturday night with thoughts about Monday?* You can zap the fun right out of a dinner party simply by yammering on and on about work. Who among us doesn't want to slap the loudmouth who won't stop talking about his recent promotion?

But not artists. True artists don't want to separate work from life. Instead, they weave work and life together into a unified whole, *and they love it.* You see, artists know a secret: people were created to work not in order to survive or earn money but for the sheer joy of it. Work is a creative expression of who and what we are—image-bearers of the Creator. God designed work to be a form of worship, and we experience great gobs of joy when our worship, work, and life are all one. To this end, Dorothy Sayers writes:

> The first thing he [the author of the Bible] tells us about God, in whose image both man and woman were created, is that He was Himself a Creator. He made things. Not presumably because He had to, but because He wanted to. . . . Man is a maker, who makes things because he wants to, because he cannot fulfill his true nature if he is prevented from making things for the love of the job; he is

made in the image of the Maker, and he must himself create or become something less than a man.[19]

That idealistic image of work—a creative act of joyful worship—is all fine, if you want to starve. It's no mystery why many artists are skinny and live in a rented closet: creating things "for the love of the job" often means creating things nobody will buy. Somehow, the rest of us find it impossible to reconcile fuzzy ideas about "working for the sheer joy of it" with the cost of raising our kids and repairing our minivans.

Work as worship seems to be a pre-fall image of work. Before the fall, our purpose was clear—have dominion, fill the earth, and subdue it. God established humans as rulers of the earth. Back in those days, Adam and Eve never doubted their significance. They never tried to create an identity for themselves. They never freaked out because they might miss God's call on their lives, and they never divided their lives into sacred and secular compartments. Before the fall, Adam and Eve never struggled with vocational guilt. Additionally, all of their physical needs were freely met. If they were hungry, they simply reached out and picked a big, juicy peach or some other scrumptious fruit.

Under those pre-fall conditions, it's easy to see how work was purely worship—a continuous reflection of God's glory through our creative activity. Humankind didn't have to work in order to eat. We worked purely as an act of expressing the Creator's image; we reflected God by shaping the earth. Adam and Eve didn't work

---

[19] Dorothy L. Sayers, "Vocation in Work," in *A Christian Basis for the Post-War World*, ed. Albert E. Baker (London: Student Christian Movement Press, 1942), 89.

to live; they lived to work, because work was worship. Life, work, and worship were all one.

After the fall, work became an economic necessity. We are no longer free to work for the sheer joy of it. We must work, instead, to live. "Work is worship" rings hollow in our post-fall ears. *Work is worship? Yeah, right.* Our perception of work is massively distorted by the cursed reality of Monday mornings. Adam and Eve twisted the image of God by attempting to create their own, autonomous identity apart from God. They worshiped themselves rather than God. This, of course, was the ultimate human screwup. Now we're all in a mess: We're plagued by horrific confusion over our identity. We're not sure why we're on this planet. Books on discovering God's call are wildly popular, and many of us struggle with vocational guilt.

Many of today's artists simply opt out of the post-fall system. They work to an idealistic, pre-fall standard. They live to work rather than work to live. They may be skinny and living in a rented closet, but they're passionate about their work; creative energy flows out of their souls. They know the secret. The fundamental, pre-fall truth about work—work is worship—never changed; it's still true today, after the fall. It turns out that working for the sheer, worshipful joy of it, rather than to pay bills, is the key to loving your job.

Nowhere in the Bible does God change the purpose of our work. It is still meant to be worship. This pre-fall truth was not broken or canceled by the fall. It was, rather, choked from our view by thistles, thorns, and economic necessity. Work was cursed, but our divine mandate never changed. We are to have dominion, fill the earth, and subdue it. You and I are still hard-wired to organize, build, and manage—to create. It's an essential element of who and what God made us to be—his image-bearers. But now we must bear that image through a torrent of blood, sweat, and tears.

Work *Is* Worship

People generally assume that marketplace work, in and of itself, has no intrinsic eternal value. Christians often speak of glorifying God *at* work but rarely *through* work. The distinction between *at* and *through* is subtle but telling. Glorifying God *at* work assumes our work is a good platform for ministry but is itself empty of intrinsic value. For example, it's common to hear a sermon praising work as a means to ministry—*be a good testimony, work hard, do excellent work, be honest, witness to your coworkers, earn money to support kingdom work.* These admonitions are all good and needed, but there's far more to our work than merely being a platform.

Within this work-as-platform framework, marketplace vocations are tolerated, because they are necessary to enable the truly significant work of ministry. In other words, marketplace work doesn't glorify God directly, but it enables God-glorifying ministry. The truck driver sitting nine pews back, third from the left can't help but see the obvious ranking of vocations.

But God designed marketplace work as part of the very essence and purpose of humankind. Therefore, it glorifies God directly, intrinsically. We glorify God not only at work, but also through the actual work itself. It is intrinsically valuable. It is significant. Though burdened with decay, frustration, and pain, our everyday labor reflects the glory of our Creator. It is a fundamental element in our tiny aurora glimmer of his infinite majesty and worth. It is an act of worship.

The Object of Work's Worship

Most of us have a tough time accepting the bizarre claim that work is worship. An important clarification will help: all work is worship, but not all work worships God. Much of it worships self rather than God; it is idolatry, and God hates it. This is equally true of both marketplace work and ministry work. As a guest speaker, I can stand in front of a congregation and preach a sermon for the glory of myself, not God. Artists can work for the glory of themselves, not God. The same is true of biologists, whitewater rafting guides, evangelists, and doctors; this fact is true of all professions. The object of work's worship—God or self—does not hinge on the work being done. It hinges, rather, on the heart of the worker.

In the Bible, the apostle Paul told a group of marketplace workers, "Whatever you do, work heartily, as for the Lord. . . . You are serving the Lord Christ."[20] In stark contrast, Jesus repeatedly lambasted full-time ministry workers, because "They do all their deeds to be seen by others."[21] He called them hypocrites, children of hell, blind guides, whitewashed tombs, and a brood of vipers.[22] "This people honors me with their lips, but their heart is far from me; in vain do they worship me."[23] The problem wasn't their work, whether it was sacred or secular; the problem was their hearts.

---

[20] Colossians 3:23–24
[21] Matthew 23:5
[22] Matthew 23:13, 15–16, 27, 33
[23] Matthew 15:8–9

There's far more to worship than work, because there's far more to life than work. We live all of life, not just work, from the heart. The Bible says, "Keep your heart with all vigilance, for from it flow the springs of life."[24] God intends that all of life should be an act of worship. Every day, every second, and every mundane task is a living reflection of his glory. God's purpose for our lives didn't change after the fall. He demands our all—nothing less. Our physical, practical, everyday lives are meant to be our living sacrifices—our acts of spiritual worship. The apostle Paul wrote, "I appeal to you therefore, brothers, by the mercies of God, to present your bodies as a living sacrifice, holy and acceptable to God, which is your spiritual worship."[25]

The lowliest task, done as an act of worship, embodies the highest purpose. Some Christian authors argue that degrading, loathsome, apparently meaningless jobs couldn't possibly be part of God's plan to magnify his glory. And millions of us couldn't agree more—especially on Monday mornings. But the Bible says even bondservants should do their work "with a sincere heart . . . as servants of Christ, doing the will of God from the heart, rendering service with a good will as to the Lord."[26] A bondservant was essentially an impoverished person who sold himself into slavery to avoid starvation. There could hardly be a lowlier job. Yet there is no higher purpose or greater significance than the reflection of God's glory—"doing the will of God from the heart . . . as to the Lord."

Those bondservants almost certainly longed for better jobs—a transition from slavery to success. But they needed no transition

---

[24] Proverbs 4:23
[25] Romans 12:1
[26] Ephesians 6:5–7

from slavery (or success) to significance. Their significance was secure; it was embodied in the person and work of Jesus Christ.
Their lives were bound in slavery, but their hearts were free to
work "as for the Lord." The tyranny of slavery could not rob them
of their identity or their everlasting worth. Their lives were living
sacrifices—acts of spiritual worship. On Monday mornings, you
and I don't need to pretend our work is sheer joy and heavenly
bliss. It's not. It is, however, an act of spiritual worship.

Worship All Seven Days

By far, we will expend the largest portion of our lives—our living
sacrifices—at work, not church. God could have easily established
six days of sabbath and one day of work, but he didn't. "Six days
you shall labor."[27] Man's chief end is to glorify God, and that end
isn't restricted to just one out of seven days each week. Please don't
misunderstand me. Attending church is a vital part of worship and
an integral part of our life in the body of Christ. Outdoor enthusi-
asts sometimes tell me, "I don't need to go to church. The great
outdoors is my church; that's where I worship God." That senti-
ment is just plain wrong, because the God they claim to be worshiping commands us to go to church with other people[28] and
submit to the authority of a pastor.[29] There is, however, far more
to worship than church—six days more.

Work, church, and life are all woven together into our living
sacrifice—our worship. We err when we single out either work or
church as more or less significant than the other. When we play

---

27 Exodus 20:9
28 Deuteronomy 31:12–13, Hebrews 10:25
29 Hebrews 13:17

that game, we miss the whole point. The point is not to glorify work or church. The point (of it all) is to glorify God.

In 1972, Pulitzer Prize-winning author Studs Terkel captured the interwoven relationship between work and church when he interviewed Nick Lindsay, a 44-year-old carpenter who "started workin' steady at it when I was thirteen. I picked up a hammer and went to drive in nails." Lindsay reflected:

> You work like you were kneeling down. You go into Riverside Church in New York and there's no space between the pews to kneel. (Laughs.) If you try to kneel down in that church, you break your nose on the pew in front. A bunch of churches are like that. Who kneels down in that church? I'll tell you who kneels. The man kneels who's settin' the toilets in the restroom. He's got to kneel, that's part of his work. The man who nails the pews on the floor, he had to kneel down. The man who put the receptacles in the walls that turn that I-don't-know-how-many horsepower organ they got in that Riverside Church—that thing'll blow you halfway to heaven right away, *pow!*—the man who was putting the wires in that thing, he kneeled down. Any work, you kneel down—it's a kind of worship. It's part of the holiness of things, work, yes.[30]

Today, we eat bread by the sweat of our face. But it will not always be so. The curse will be lifted, and we will once again make

---

[30] Terkel, *Working*, 517–518.

things "for the love of the job." We will organize, build, manage, and create. But we'll do these things with unbridled joy for the glory of our Maker. Until then, you and I can face the daily grind knowing our eternal significance is secure in him. Therefore, "Let us offer to God acceptable worship, with reverence and awe."[31] On Monday as well as on Sunday.

THE MANDATE DISPUTE

We just spent several pages talking about our divine mandate to "have dominion, fill the earth, and subdue it."[32] But we didn't mention our *other* divine mandate—the Great Commission: "Go therefore and make disciples of all nations, baptizing them in the name of the Father and of the Son and of the Holy Spirit, teaching them to observe all that I have commanded you."[33]

We have one God and one Bible, but it seems like we have two big mandates—the creation mandate (have dominion, fill, and subdue) and the Great Commission (go and make disciples). Which is more important? Which should be the focus of the church? Which is more eternally significant? Theological disputes rage, tempers flare, battle lines are drawn, churches split, and entire denominations line up behind one mandate or the other. Within churches that strongly emphasize the Great Commission, many Christians feel waves of vocational guilt, because their work seems to be a lesser calling, a secular calling; it's not part of God's central mission in the world.

---

[31] Hebrews 12:28
[32] Genesis 1:26, 28
[33] Matthew 28:19–20

The entire dispute is nonsense. We don't have two independent mandates. The creation mandate and the Great Commission are two aspects of the ultimate mandate, the cover-to-cover mandate of the Bible: *magnify the glory of God.* We err hugely when we set the creation mandate and the Great Commission at odds with each other. It's like pitting your foot against your hand and endlessly debating which is more important. (I can picture Bubba scratching his belly right now.) When we separate these mandates and assign eternal significance to only one or the other, we fragment our lives. Our days shatter into shards of sacred and secular, higher and lower, significant and insignificant. We typically align marketplace work with the creation mandate and ministry work with the Great Commission. But in the Bible, it's not that simple.

Remember, our hearts determine whom we worship *through* our work. This is a serious problem, because you and I are born with hearts bent toward worshiping ourselves, not God. The Bible says we have hearts of stone. Our hearts are stone-dead. Actually, they're worse than dead. Our hearts hurl us toward an eternity in hell. There's only one way to get a heart that is alive, a heart that worships God. God must give it to us. "I will give you a new heart, and a new spirit I will put within you. And I will remove the heart of stone from your flesh. . . . You shall be my people, and I will be your God."[34]

God says he will replace our dead hearts with new, living hearts by the means of our hearing his Word, the gospel. "Faith comes from hearing, and hearing through the word of Christ."[35] So we need to get out there and proclaim the gospel so that others

---

[34] Ezekiel 36:26, 28
[35] Romans 10:17

may hear it and receive new hearts. This is the work of the Great Commission.

However, the Great Commission doesn't nullify the creation mandate. Instead, it extends it. As we've seen, the creation mandate (have dominion, fill, and subdue) is a mandate to worship, and our fulfillment of it is an act of worship. In other words, work is worship, even after the fall. Rather than nullify this act of worship, the Great Commission extends it in two ways. First, it adds the new task, "Make disciples," as part of having dominion, filling the earth, and subduing it. Second, it is the means by which God transforms each new disciple's fulfillment of the creation mandate into an act of God-worship rather than self-worship.

Through his Word, God will replace hearts of stone with living hearts. These new hearts will change work's object of worship from *self* to *God*. Hence, among all the nations, God's people will fulfill the creation mandate for the praise, worship, and glory of God alone. In the end, both mandates work in unison to exalt God's glory. In a sense, we could say that the Great Commission reaffirms the creation mandate within the context of a fallen world. By sharing the gospel, we can make disciples and fill the earth with God-glorifying people whose work of having dominion over the earth and subduing it is once again an act of God-worship.

The Mandates United in Victory

The Bible binds these two mandates together as part of God's final victory over Satan. Creation will be redeemed. God will "reconcile to himself all things,"[36] thereby stripping Satan of his treasonous

---

[36] Colossians 1:20

reign over all the earth. At the end of this age—this time of war—Jesus Christ will lay final claim to his inheritance; the redeemed earth will be his forevermore. Francis Schaeffer writes, "Not only will believing mankind be redeemed, but all creation will be redeemed along with them. Satan will not be allowed a victory in the world of humans, and Satan will not be allowed a victory in the world of the total creation."[37]

The blood of Jesus Christ purchased the eternal redemption of both humankind and creation. We see this in Romans 8:19–24, where we find two truths that surprise many of today's Christians. First, God will resurrect and redeem all of creation, not just the bodies of believers. Second, creation will be redeemed and resurrected *through* (because of) the resurrection of believers.

> For the creation waits with eager longing for the revealing of the sons of God. For the creation was subjected to futility, not willingly, but because of him who subjected it, in hope that the creation itself will be set free from its bondage to corruption and obtain the freedom of the glory of the children of God. For we know that the whole creation has been groaning together in the pains of childbirth until now. And not only the creation, but we ourselves, who have the firstfruits of the Spirit, groan inwardly as we wait eagerly for adoption as sons, the redemption of our bodies. For in this hope we were saved. (Romans 8:19–24)

---

[37] Francis A. Schaeffer, *The Finished Work of Christ: The Truth of Romans 1–8* (Wheaton, IL: Crossway, 1998), 215.

God subjected creation to the curse *because* of humankind, and one day, he will set creation free from the curse *through* humankind. At the fall, we totally botched our God-given responsibility over creation—our divine creation mandate to be God's earth-shapers. Yet it's still our responsibility; it's still our mandate. And because creation is entrusted to our care and dominion, its future and eternal glory are forever bound to our future and eternal glory.

Here is where the Great Commission leaps onto center stage alongside the creation mandate. You and I are bound for *hell,* not glory, unless we are children of God (people with God-worshiping hearts). Which means God's creation project, entrusted to our stewardship through the creation mandate, is also bound for hell unless God transforms our stone-dead human hearts through the Great Commission. Thus the mandates are intricately bound together in God's ultimate victory and the reconciliation of all things to himself.

The Future of the Mandates

Two important questions now arise: what becomes of our two divine mandates *after* the resurrection, and how can creation be redeemed if it will be annihilated by a great fire in the last days? Matthew Henry answered these questions in his exposition of Romans:

> The fire at the last day shall be a refining, not a destroying annihilating fire. . . . For, as it was with man and for man that [every created thing] fell under the curse, so with man and for man they

shall be delivered. All the curse and filth that now adhere to the creature shall be done away then when those that have suffered with Christ upon earth shall reign with him upon the earth.[38]

With a refining fire, God will purge creation of all that is evil. Then he will renew creation in a stunning display of his glory—"a new heaven and a new earth."[39] The work of the Great Commission will be done. Its time will end. However, our first mandate, the creation mandate, will continue into eternity. We will reign over the earth as "heirs—heirs of God and fellow heirs with Christ."[40] The elders of heaven will sing a new song to the Lamb, the Son of God: "Worthy are you . . . for you were slain, and by your blood you ransomed people for God from every tribe and language and people and nation, and you have made them a kingdom and priests to our God, and they shall reign on the earth."[41]

We deserve hell. "But God, being rich in mercy, because of the great love with which he loved us, even when we were dead in our trespasses, made us alive together with Christ."[42] Not only does God redeem our souls, but he also redeems our bodies, and then he redeems creation through us. As part of his ultimate redemption of creation, he redeems our regular, everyday work. For through it, you and I have shaped creation—we have created, filled, and subdued. Finally, as if all of this were not enough, God

---

[38] Matthew Henry, *Commentary on the Whole Bible: Complete and Unabridged in One Volume* (Peabody, MA: Hendrickson, 1991, *Logos Bible Software,* Bellingham, WA: Logos, 2009).
[39] Revelation 21:1
[40] Romans 8:17
[41] Revelation 5:9–10; see also Revelation 22:5, ". . . they will reign forever and ever."
[42] Ephesians 2:4–5

will once again install us as his royal regents, kings and queens of the earth, stewards at the bequest of our great emperor. Our response can only be awestruck worship. "And I heard every creature in heaven and on earth and under the earth and in the sea, and all that is in them, saying, 'To him who sits on the throne and to the Lamb be blessing and honor and glory and might forever and ever!'"[43]

"This is the song of redeemed creation," writes Schaeffer, "not even just every animated thing, but every created thing. . . . There will be a day when, once again, the 'morning stars will sing together' just as they did at creation."[44] Therefore, missionaries, go! Go and reach the nations; do it with all your might. And marketplace laborers, work! Have dominion, fill the earth, and subdue it; do it with all your might.

In summary, marketplace work enables ministry, but then ministry work loops back around and enables all of our work to be God-centered worship. Both types of work are intrinsically significant. Both directly glorify God. Both are totally dependent on "the word of his power."[45] And both are bound together in eternal redemption and God's final victory over Satan. So then, which type of work—which mandate—is more important to God? Nonsense. The answer is nonsense, because the question is a nonsense question; the entire dispute is a nonsense dispute. Our divine mandate is clear—*do them both with all your might.*

---

[43] Revelation 5:13
[44] Schaeffer, *The Finished Work of Christ*, 217.
[45] Hebrews 1:3

SERVING TWO MASTERS

Do you serve two different masters (God and money) when you work as a telephone lineman all day and then lead a Bible study at church in the evening? Did Daniel serve two masters when he worked for Babylon all day and then prayed at his house in the evening? Not a chance. We, like Daniel, serve one master or the other, not both. Our hearts, not the classification of our jobs, determine whom we serve. "No one can serve two masters, for either he will hate the one and love the other, or he will be devoted to the one and despise the other. You cannot serve God and money."[46]

When we compartmentalize our lives, and in effect, build a dividing wall between the sacred and secular sides of life, we are double-minded. We wind up doubting the eternal value of our work and thus our lives, because we're torn between two masters. As a result, many of us struggle with a vague sense of guilt, because we fear we are serving the false god of money during our working hours. In the end, however, our doubt, guilt, and fear are all for naught, because the dividing wall between sacred and secular is not real. It is a figment of our imagination—"a creature of misunderstanding."[47] There simply is no sacred-secular divide in life; there is only life. And your heart determines its master.

But when we think back to what we learned in Sunday school, it's really hard to say there's no divide or wall between the sacred and the secular. After all, in Sunday school, we learned a bunch of strange Bible stories about Old Testament priests, temple ceremonies, and the terrifying Holy of Holies. Back in Old Testament

---

[46] Matthew 6:24
[47] Tozer, *The Pursuit of God*, 111.

days, there was a literal wall—a great veil—between the Holy of Holies and the outside world, between the sacred and the secular. God allowed only the priests to pass through that veil, so they clearly had a more significant job than everyone else—right? A. W. Tozer guides us out of this quandary when he writes:

> There were holy days, holy vessels, holy garments. There were washings, sacrifices, offerings of many kinds. By these means Israel learned that God is holy. It was this that He was teaching them. Not the holiness of things or places, but the holiness of Jehovah was the lesson they must learn.
>
> Then came the great day when Christ appeared.... The Old Testament schooling was over. When Christ died on the cross the veil of the temple was rent from top to bottom. The Holy of Holies was opened to everyone who would enter in faith.[48]

The blood-soaked cry of Jesus, "Eli, Eli, lema sabachthani,"[49] tore the veil in two; it demolished the wall between sacred and secular. Yet two thousand years later, we believe pastors are more significant to God than truck drivers. We've rebuilt the fallen wall. We've heaped up rubble stained with the blood of the infinite.

When Jesus died on the cross, he created a whole new priest-hood—you and me. The Bible says Jesus Christ "has freed us from our sins by his blood and made us a kingdom, priests to his God and Father."[50] You and I are now the priests of God. We are priests,

---

[48] Tozer, *The Pursuit of God,* 115–116.
[49] Matthew 27:46
[50] Revelation 1:5–6

not with flowing robes and ornate scepters, but with hard hats, cell phones, stethoscopes, computers, and steel-toe boots. The Holy of Holies is no longer a veiled room containing a golden box and the stone tablets of God's law. It is, rather, our hearts. "This is the covenant that I will make with them after those days, declares the Lord: I will put my laws on their hearts."[51] He changed our hearts to be living hearts. He made us his royal priests, and he promises to return one day and raise us up with him.

No one but God knows the day and the hour of his future return, but Jesus gave some examples of the kind of work we'll be doing when he comes to raise us up with him. Interestingly, he didn't use examples of ministry work. Instead, he said, "Two men will be in the field; one will be taken and one left. Two women will be grinding at the mill; one will be taken and one left."[52]

Two people will be doing the exact same regular, everyday work—secular work. One has a heart of stone; the other is an heir with Christ and a member of his royal priesthood. One will receive the sentence of eternal horror: "I never knew you; depart from me."[53] The other will receive the gift of eternal blessing: "Enter into the joy of your master."[54]

With living hearts, we are servants of Christ. Some of us will work in ministry jobs; most of us will work in marketplace jobs. Either way, our purpose is clear. We are to fill the earth with the glory of God, our Master—our *only* Master.

Paradigm-shattering? Absolutely. It's wall-shattering.

---

[51] Hebrews 10:16
[52] Matthew 24:40–41
[53] Matthew 7:23
[54] Matthew 25:21

CHAPTER 9

OUR SPHERES OF LABOR

God gives the wool, but not without our labor. If it is on the sheep, it makes no garment.

—Martin Luther[1]

The artist desiring to paint a picture, the engineer desiring to build a bridge, the housewife desiring to bake a cake—each must do more than mere thinking and willing. Action must flow.

—Francis Schaeffer[2]

If a man marries his housekeeper, the gross national product will fall. The paid labor of the housekeeper is replaced by the unmarketed [free] service of the wife.

—Juliet B. Schor[3]

---

[1] Luther, quoted in Wingren, *Luther On Vocation,* 8.
[2] Francis A. Schaeffer, *No Little People* (Wheaton, IL: Crossway, 2003), 34.
[3] Schor, *The Overworked American,* 85.

Our left wingtip slammed into the ground. The landing gear of the two-seat Piper Cub collapsed underneath us, and we lurched to a crunching stop on the side of a mountain.

No blood, no pain, no injuries. It could have been worse, a lot worse. So far, so good—but we were stuck on a mountain in the middle of the Wrangell-Saint Elias wilderness with a busted airplane, and the weather was closing in fast.

The game plan was for the pilot to drop me off on the mountainside above tree-line. There I would set up a base camp and then spend the next five days climbing the surrounding peaks. But the sides of wilderness mountains aren't typically equipped with paved airport runways. Instead, they offer an occasional patch of smooth turf and rock that isn't too steep. These landing spots are tiny and uneven but big enough for the best bush pilots in Alaska to land and drop off an amateur mountain climber like me.

If only we had seen that little hollow in the ground. It was small—maybe two feet wide and a foot deep—an inexplicable depression in the ground that seemed to have no reason for being there other than to swallow our left tire at the precise instant we touched down. Our right tire landed on firm ground; the left dipped into the hollow. Then everything went wrong in a hurry.

As we stood on the side of the mountain, pondering our predicament, we suddenly heard the sound of heaven. No, we didn't hear angels singing the "Hallelujah Chorus"; rather, we heard the sound of another airplane—another Piper Cub, to be precise.

In a flash, we were on the radio with the other pilot. He circled in close to see the damage; then he disappeared into the horizon. An hour and a half later, he was back. This time, though, he had the repair supplies we needed, and he had a buddy with him to help. While flying in low circles over our heads, they dropped the supplies to us through the window of the plane—tools, parts, and even a five-foot length of two-by-four to use as a makeshift lever. (Anyone familiar with the cramped cockpit of a Piper Cub will understand the *wow!* of this feat.) My pilot and I got to work, and two hours later, with only minutes of daylight remaining, our patched-together airplane was back in the air, headed for home.

In our mountainside hour of need, God could have sent us angels, but he didn't. He sent us a guy with an airplane, a two-by-four, and the flying skills necessary to help us.

Life is full of surprise hollows, busted landing gear, and approaching storms. God could bail us out of our troubles with a single word or a host of angels. But mostly, he doesn't. Instead, he sends Bob, Gary, Sue, Dave, Jennifer—regular, everyday people just like you and me. And he sends different people to meet different needs. It snowed last night in the valley where I live, so someone got up early this morning and plowed the roads. No one in official Christian ministry plowed the roads. Steve, a buddy of mine who works for the Department of Transportation, plowed the roads. Kids went to school, adults went to work, friends met for coffee—lives were shaped, lives that have no ending, because Steve got up and drove the snowplow this morning. Steve shaped today—and he shaped eternity.

The bewildering flood of vocational guilt among today's Christians demands a restatement of the plain truth: God, in his infinite wisdom, primarily chooses to work in this world through means, and *you* are the means. You and I represent a mind-boggling variety of vocations. We each live, relate, and work in our own unique time and place. Through this boundless variety, God sustains the world. People can't wear wool coats unless someone sheers the sheep. People can't eat southern-style barbecue unless someone cooks a pig to perfection (twelve hours over hickory logs). People can't type books on a computer unless someone develops the word processing software. We each have our own labor. That's the plain truth—and it shapes eternity.

Martin Luther often said we are the means and mask of God. In the following statement, Luther is referring to the regular, everyday tasks of "our work in the field, in the garden, in the city, in the home, in struggle, in government." "These are the masks of our Lord God, behind which he wants to be hidden and to do all things. . . . God bestows all that is good on us, but you must stretch out your hands and lay hold of the horns of the bull, i.e. you must work and lend yourself as a means and a mask to God."[4]

Of the seven billion people on this planet, you are the only one who fills your unique sphere of work, roles, and relationships. Steve plowed our roads this morning—nobody else. The guy with an airplane and a two-by-four saved us on the mountain—nobody else. For the rest of eternity, nobody else will ever stand in your particular place in this epic war. God gave you a role to fill. Maybe it's nine rows back, third from the left, but he gave it to you and nobody else.

---

[4] Luther, quoted in Wingren, *Luther On Vocation*, 137–138.

Whether you work in the ministry or in the marketplace, you are the means and mask of God. He is the one who forges today and forever, but he does it, in part, through your work, roles, and relationships. There is no room for human pride in this astonishing wonder; neither is there any room for vocational guilt. God, in his infinite wisdom, primarily chooses to work in this world through means, and *you* are the means.

WE ALL EXPERIENCE THE VOCATIONAL GUILT OF A SOLDIER

Grizzly bears have huge claws—four-inch rippers that kill moose, caribou, and sometimes people. But God, in his sustaining providence, gave humankind a group of hard-working people who earn their daily bread in a manufacturing company called Remington Arms. Consequently, when I come across a bear in the Alaskan wilderness, I don't pray, *"Dear Lord, save me!"* Instead, I pray, "Dear Lord, thank you for the food my family and I are about to receive. Amen." Bear stew is a favorite at our house. (And for those who are wondering: bolt action Model 700, chambered in .300 Remington Ultra Mag.)

You and I live in a fallen world—a world plagued by sin, death, and decay—a world at war. We grind through days of constant struggle. Even the little stuff in life weighs us down. Minivans blow head gaskets, knee joints degenerate, water pipes corrode and leak, and financial reports confound us. But God, in his sustaining providence, gave us auto mechanics, orthopedic surgeons, plumbers, and financial advisors. The battles get worse, though—much worse. In this fallen world, political dictators brutalize their people, regimes commit genocide, tyrants oppress the weak, and extremists terrorize the innocent.

You'd think we hardly need to say another word. The legitimacy and significance of the soldier's vocation seems all too obvious. However, within some Christian circles, there flows an underlying current of antipathy for the military profession. Their line of reasoning assumes that since the soldier's vocation is rooted in violence, it must therefore be fundamentally wrong. At a minimum, the position is a necessary evil; the soldier certainly disobeys God's command to love our enemies. Hearing this, it's no wonder that a few soldiers periodically struggle with a unique form of vocational guilt. They think, *Am I wasting my life in a career that seems necessary on a human level but is actually wrong in God's eyes?*

I want to spend a few pages focusing specifically on the soldier's vocation for two reasons. First, in the United States alone, nearly five million people work in the military or in law enforcement professions.[5] Second, everyone, you and I included, must periodically enforce justice to some degree in the routine course of daily life—but many of us feel a little bit guilty about it. This isn't just the guilt of a soldier or law enforcement officer. This guilt is a menace to all of us, because all of us must occasionally discipline, confront, reprimand, and punish others. You and I carry the responsibility to administer justice whether we're flight attendants, pastors, dentists, coffeehouse baristas, or moms. We live in a world of thistles and thorns. Vendors cheat us, coworkers shirk their responsibilities, customers breach contracts, and kids push their

---

[5] "Occupational Outlook Handbook," last modified March 29, 2012, http://www.bls.gov/ooh/military/military-careers.htm; and http://www.bls.gov/ooh/protective-service/home.htm.

boundaries. And in some small way, we also experience the vocational guilt of a soldier.

But what about the inherent nature of enforcing justice or punishing others? Doesn't it defy everything the Bible says about loving our enemies and trusting God to be our avenger? The Bible seems to be at total odds with the sword, especially when we read passages like these: "Beloved, never avenge yourselves, but leave it to the wrath of God, for it is written, 'Vengeance is mine, I will repay, says the Lord.' To the contrary, if your enemy is hungry, feed him; if he is thirsty, give him something to drink. . . . Do not be overcome by evil, but overcome evil with good."[6] "But I say to you who hear, Love your enemies, do good to those who hate you, bless those who curse you, pray for those who abuse you. To one who strikes you on the cheek, offer the other also."[7]

How could any Christian read those passages and still serve as a soldier, policeman, SWAT team sniper, prosecuting attorney, or FBI agent? It seems like Jesus wants us to hug the bad guys and buy them hamburgers for dinner. I once knew a soldier who latched onto these passages and became convinced they were God's unconditional, final ruling against violence. He eventually left the military and grew so passionate in his newfound conviction that he told me, "If a burglar breaks into my house, hurts my child, and tries to rape my wife, it would be wrong of me to use violent force to stop him." That soldier was confused by a profound misunderstanding.

Yes, God is a God of mercy. He commands us to love our enemies, because in showing mercy, we show the world what God is like. However, God is also a God of justice—fierce, violent jus-

---

[6] Romans 12:19–21
[7] Luke 6:27–29

tice. Read the rest of the Bible. It's one of the bloodiest books on the shelves of your local bookstore. Throughout the Bible, God leads his people into ferocious battles. When Jesus returns, he will be armed with a sword, not hugs and hamburgers. "He will tread the winepress of the fury of the wrath of God the Almighty."[8] The blood of his enemies will flow from the winepress "as high as a horse's bridle."[9] God's holiness is absolute, and he will justly defend his holiness in absolute measure.

You and I are on this earth to reflect the glory of God. We do this by upholding not only his mercy, but also his justice. Several Christians in the early New Testament church were military officers. "At Caesarea there was a man named Cornelius, a centurion . . . a devout man who feared God."[10] When a group of soldiers asked John the Baptist how they could best "bear fruits in keeping with repentance,"[11] John didn't tell them to make the transition into ministry. Rather, he told them not to abuse their power for personal gain and to be content with their wages.[12] In other words, he told them to continue being soldiers and to be honorable soldiers. Martin Luther once observed, "If the waging of war and the military profession were in themselves wrong and displeasing to God, we would have to condemn Abraham, Moses, Joshua, David, and all the rest of the holy fathers, kings, and princes who served God as soldiers and are highly praised in Scripture."[13]

---

[8] Revelation 19:15
[9] Revelation 14:20
[10] Acts 10:1–2
[11] Luke 3:8
[12] Luke 3:14
[13] Martin Luther, "Whether Soldiers, Too, Can Be Saved," In *Callings: Twenty Centuries of Christian Wisdom on Vocation,* edited by William C. Placher (Grand Rapids: William B. Eerdmans, 2005), 220.

We're caught in a dilemma: do we turn the other cheek, or do we blow our enemy to smithereens? The key to solving this puzzle is to step back and see the distinction between the *individual* and the individual's *office*—between the person and the role the person fills. Luther said, "We must distinguish between an occupation and the man who holds it."[14] This distinction is critical, because it draws a line between the individual's desire for personal vengeance and the individual's responsibility as spouse, soldier, policeman, attorney, judge, or even executioner.

These offices serve and uphold various *God-ordained* institutions. The Bible clearly reveals that God established the institutions of family, state, business, and church. They are part of his sustaining providence—blessings he gives to us for the good of humankind and all creation. Humans didn't invent family, state, business, and church. God did, and he means to be glorified in each of these institutions.

Here's the catch: if those institutions abandon justice and only show mercy, they will cease to exist. They will collapse. Without a strong foundation of accountability, boundaries, and discipline—without a foundation of justice—homes disintegrate, businesses fail, churches implode, and nations succumb to tyranny. If parents set no boundaries and enforce no rules in the home—well, we've all seen what happens, and it isn't pretty. If businesses forgive every breach of trust and enforce standards only rarely—if mercy becomes the norm and justice the exception—they will soon collapse under the weight of poor quality and corruption. Institutions must stand on justice or die. Therefore, our foundational duty in serving our institutions (fulfilling our offices) is justice, not mercy.

---

14 Luther, "Whether Soldiers, Too, Can Be Saved," In *Callings,* 218.

God ordains the institutions, and God ordains the justice that up-holds those institutions.

Additionally, without justice, there is no mercy. Mercy itself stands on the foundation of justice. We see this best in the life-giving truth of the gospel. God's mercy (salvation through the blood of Jesus Christ) stands on the foundation of his absolute holiness and justice (the infinite demand of the cross). In a sense, we can say God's mercy flows from his justice. Likewise, human mercy is only visible against the backdrop of unwavering justice. If we were to abandon justice and fixate exclusively on Jesus' com-mands in the Sermon on the Mount—to turn the other cheek, be merciful, and to not resist evil—then only criminals would sur-vive. Human society would soon end in bloody chaos. In response to this grim quandary, Martin Luther once said (here paraphrased by scholar Gustaf Wingren), "The temporal sword sees to it that things do not go that way. Because there is rigorous government, man can take the Sermon on the Mount in earnest."[15]

The office of the sword secures the foundation from which we are free to show mercy. As individuals, you and I must turn the other cheek and love our enemies. We dare not seek our own per-sonal vengeance; rather, we leave it to God. But in our offices and our roles, we must bear the sword—the God-ordained, violent sword. Through it, God protects and sustains humankind. So hus-bands, if a burglar breaks into your house and threatens your fam-ily, *tear his head off!* Do it with all your might! And solders, *fight,* because you are the sword of justice—the foundation of mercy. Gustaf Wingren said, "The paradox rests with God: it is *he* who forcibly resists evil through the offices of judge and executioner,

---

15 Wingren, *Luther on Vocation,* 8.

and commands all persons not to resist evil as individuals, even though they be judges and executioners. For that which the office does is not part of man's account, but of God's."[16]

We each have an office to fulfill. It's part of our God-given vocation. We are called to administer a basic standard of justice in our unique spheres of work, roles, and relationships. Confrontation and discipline are never fun; most of us, if sane, dread those aspects of our duty. Yet deep inside, many of us feel something far worse than dread—we feel guilt. It's as if enforcing justice is somehow a bit sinful. We wonder, *Aren't we supposed to be like Jesus and show unconditional mercy?* That uncertainty eventually leads to guilt. But that guilt, the vocational guilt of a soldier, is a lie.

LETTING GO OF SOME BAGGAGE

To save a ship caught in a storm, the crew will pitch the cargo overboard. I once pitched my backpack, containing fifty pounds of gear, over the edge of a two hundred foot cliff. I was trapped on a ledge and couldn't climb to safety with all that extra weight on my back. You've done some pitching in your life, too—maybe not over the edge of a ship or a cliff, but from time to time, we must all let go of some baggage or else get pulled into the abyss. Today, many of us are loaded down with lifelong assumptions about our vocations—assumptions that drag us into the abyss of vocational guilt. It's time to pitch them.

Our goal in the remaining sections of this chapter is to pitch four assumptions overboard. The first is that the Bible says pastors are worthy of "double honor," so they must be more significant

---

16 Wingren, *Luther on Vocation,* 8.

than the rest of us. The second is that the Bible says people in full-time ministry have a higher calling than everyone else. The third is that only "the Lord's work" counts for eternity. The fourth is that the Bible story of Mary and Martha teaches us that spiritual devotion is superior to busy, everyday temporal activity.

If we totally ignore the context of these Bible passages, then yes, the Bible really does say a few of those things. The trouble is that when we rip these passages out of context, we totally misapply them. We use them to measure the eternal significance of our vocations (and our lives), but God gave them to us for a completely different purpose. It's similar to using a tool for something it was never intended to do. We're trying to wash the car with a chainsaw and doing a lot of damage in the process.

DOUBLE HONOR

I love my chainsaw. It's great for cutting firewood. But I don't wash my car with it. I love the Bible passage, "Let the elders who rule well be considered worthy of double honor."[17] But I don't measure the eternal significance of my vocation with it—and neither should you. This passage does not mean God is doubly impressed by elders. (Many churches now call them pastors.) It does not mean that elders (pastors) are doubly significant to God when compared to the rest of us. This passage has nothing to do with eternal significance.

Our level of honor for someone—whether elder, pastor, grandparent, school teacher, or president—has nothing to do with that person's level of significance to God. And our honoring them

---

[17] 1 Timothy 5:17

does not somehow boost their significance to God. People rightfully see and honor a person's office and deeds. But God looks directly at the heart, and he is no respecter of persons or offices. In his sustaining providence, God provided the church with leaders who have the assigned labor of serving and equipping us. We should therefore honor and submit to them. They are simply trying to fulfill their God-given vocations—their unique spheres of work, roles, and relationships.

Throughout the New Testament, the word *honor* sometimes means respect, and sometimes it refers to payment. By using the phrase "double honor," the apostle Paul seems to be telling us to do both—to respect our pastors and then put our money where our mouths are. The New Testament church, a brand-new institution when Paul wrote this passage, was trying to figure out how to work together as the body of Christ. Paul gave them this practical instruction to help establish the legitimacy of the pastoral office and to explain the means of sustaining that office. "Let the elders who rule well be considered worthy of double honor, especially those who labor in preaching and teaching. For the scripture says, 'You shall not muzzle an ox when it treads out the grain,' and, 'The laborer deserves his wages.'"[18]

It takes a ton of time and energy to study, preach, encourage, and guide people through the swamps of life. You and I wouldn't assemble cars or manage restaurants for free. We shouldn't expect our pastors to work for free, either. The sacred-secular divide reveals a new aspect of its own hideousness when marketplace laborers live on steady salaries and secure 401(k) plans but expect their pastors to "live by faith." The principle is clear: we should respect

---

[18] 1 Timothy 5:17–18

our pastors, and we should pay them for their labor. The "double honor" passage deals with both respect and pay. But it never implies that pastors are more significant to God than the rest of us. Chainsaws are terrible car scrubbers.

HIGHER CALLINGS

Many Christians believe that people in full-time ministry have a higher calling than the rest of us; therefore, people in full-time ministry must have a higher significance than the rest of us. But the Bible doesn't say that.

The phrase "high calling" shows up in the KJV translation of Philippians 3:14, where the apostle Paul said, "I press toward the mark for the prize of the high calling of God in Christ Jesus." The ESV translates it as "the upward call." The NIV states, "God has called me heavenward." Whether high, upward, or heavenward, the meaning of this calling is clear: the verse refers to the calling to be a Christian, the call that has heaven as its prize, the upward call to God's glory. The high calling applies equally to all of us, and it has absolutely nothing to do with being a pastor or any other type of ministry laborer.

The widespread confusion over "higher calling" stems from a different passage altogether. In his first letter to the church in Corinth, Paul made this statement: "But earnestly desire the higher gifts."[19] The Bible doesn't say pastors have a higher *calling;* it says they have a higher *gift.* And neither a higher calling nor a higher gift makes anyone more significant to God. Today, in the minds of many Christians, higher *gifts* somehow morphed into higher *call-*

---

[19] 1 Corinthians 12:31

ings, and then higher callings somehow morphed into higher *eternal significance.* Our assumptions about gifts and callings have morphed far away from the truth.

Perhaps a short tale will help us see the truth of Paul's message. Imagine there was once an architectural firm that consisted of architects, sales reps, accountants, custodial technicians, and office administrators. Its owner was both powerful and benevolent. The owner loved each one of his employees dearly. However, the firm designed buildings, so the architects in the firm clearly had the "higher gifts" (the gifts that met the firm's primary need).

In time, the owner went away on an extended journey. While he was gone, the firm's architects couldn't help but feel a little bit smug. "Surely we are the owner's most significant employees. We are, after all, meeting the firm's primary need."

Meanwhile, the other employees couldn't help but feel a little bit inferior to the architects. "True, our labor is necessary to support the architects, but surely we are much less significant in the eyes of the owner." Pride, envy, doubt, and despair began to poison the firm from within.

On a particularly stressful Monday morning, the brewing trouble finally hit the fan. The firm's employees began to argue over who had the most important gifts. The architects boasted, "This is an architectural firm, and we are the architects, so there's little doubt."

The sales reps shot back, "Ah, but you'd have no clients if it weren't for us." Then the accountants fired their volley—something about the architects going to jail for tax evasion and fraud. Round and round the salvos flew. Soon the firm was in a mess. Projects floundered, contracts were breached, revenues plummeted, tempers flared, and profits vanished. This madness continued until one day, a traveling consultant arrived to assess the whole situation.

The consultant took one look around and said, "You bunch of knuckle-heads! Don't you know that you are all members of the same firm? The firm does not consist of one gift but of many gifts. Each gift is critical to the success of the firm. Yes, you are an architectural firm, but if all of you were architects, then the entire organization would fail. As members of the same firm, you are all individually members one of another. If one member suffers, all suffer together; if one member is honored, all rejoice together.[20] So if you'd like to work in the firm's area of primary need, then fine—earnestly desire to be an architect. But you've totally misunderstood the whole point of the firm. Here's a hint—it has nothing to do with who has which gift!"

Now we come to an interesting twist to our tale. The employees were the owner's very own sons and daughters. He had ransomed each of their lives by suffering the torture of a Roman cross. These are the facts: the owner created his sons and daughters, he gave them the gifts they had, he ransomed their lives, he strategically placed each one of them in their own unique position within the firm, and each was critical to the firm's success.

The traveling business consultant reminded the employees of their owner and the facts. They all fell silent in shame. At that moment, an astonishing thing occurred: the owner—the master of the whole operation—returned. The employees all gasped and fell to their faces, but the owner smiled and told them to rise. Slowly, one by one, they reached out and touched his nail-scarred hands, and they looked into his eyes. In stammering awe, they worshiped

---

[20] Romans 12:5, 1 Corinthians 12:26

him. The employees each returned to his or her own labor, and the firm flourished forever.

Two thousand years ago, the Corinthian believers argued over who had the most important gifts in the church. Sound familiar? Their story plays out like our little tale. But instead of an architectural firm, the apostle Paul explained that believers are all members of the church, which is the body of Christ. Then Paul said, "If the whole body were an eye, where would be the sense of hearing? If the whole body were an ear, where would be the sense of smell? But as it is, God arranged the members in the body, each one of them, as he chose. If all were a single member, where would the body be? As it is, there are many parts, yet one body."[21]

For an entire chapter, Paul developed the theme of unity within the vast diversity of the body of Christ. He listed many gifts, and he explained how those gifts all depend on and serve each other. Then he ended the section abruptly with a bombshell: "Are all apostles? Are all prophets? Are all teachers? Do all work miracles? Do all possess gifts of healing? Do all speak with tongues? Do all interpret? But earnestly desire the higher gifts. And I will show you a still more excellent way."[22]

"And I will show you a still more excellent way"—huh? Paul just spent an entire chapter expounding the wide diversity of gifts within the body of Christ. Then he suddenly said, "Listen, nobody can possess all of the gifts, so if you want to work in the area of the church's primary need, then fine. Knock yourself out. But you're totally missing the whole point! It isn't about your gifts; it's about your *heart*. Impressed with your gifts? Don't be foolish. There's a more excellent way—the way of the heart, the way of love. With-

---

[21] 1 Corinthians 12:17–20
[22] 1 Corinthians 12:29–31

out a heart of love, your gifts are worthless; they are nothing." Paul then launched straight into his famous passage on love:

> If I speak in the tongues of men and of angels, but have not love, I am a noisy gong or a clanging cymbal. And if I have prophetic powers, and understand all mysteries and all knowledge, and if I have all faith, so as to move mountains, but have not love, I am nothing. If I give away all I have, and if I deliver up my body to be burned, but have not love, I gain nothing. . . . So now faith, hope, and love abide, these three; but the greatest of these is love. (1 Corinthians 13:1–3, 13)

The point is clear: Without hearts of love, we are nothing. We gain nothing. Our gifts—our vocations—are clanging cymbals. Our efforts are all for naught. We are eternally bankrupt. The person with the smallest, most obscure gift may possess a great heart of love. The person with the highest, most visible gift may possess a dead heart of stone. Before the throne of God, many will point to their "higher gifts" as proof of their eternal worth and significance. But horror will sweep over them when they hear the crushing words, "I never knew you; depart from me." Any who believe they are more significant to God because they work in the ministry rather than in the marketplace should carefully weigh Jesus' words: "On that day many will say to me, 'Lord, Lord, did we not prophesy in your name, and cast out demons in your name, and do many mighty works in your name?' And then will I declare to them, 'I never knew you; depart from me.'"[23]

---

[23] Matthew 7:22–23

Marketplace employees believe the lie, too. They believe higher *gifts* are higher *callings,* and higher *callings* lead to higher *significance*. If you ask a bank manager or a carpenter, "What are you doing for the Lord?" or "What are you doing that counts for eternity?" they'll probably tell you about teaching Sunday school, hosting Tuesday night Bible studies, sponsoring the teen outreach program, and going on a two-week mission trip to Mexico. But they probably won't say a single word about the other 90 percent of their lives—banking, carpentry, mowing the lawn, and countless other activities they do day after day and week after week.

The banker and carpenter are now in deep trouble. They've linked eternal significance to the narrow list of activities associated with the "higher calling," but for them, the higher calling can never be more than a part-time calling.

Three errors lurk within their assumption. First, it assumes that church activity is our only God-given mandate. But we've already seen how our ultimate mandate to glorify God encompasses much more than church work. Second, it assumes marketplace activity has no eternal value. In the next chapter, we will put that assumption to rest by exploring the wondrous future of our everyday work. Third, it assumes that usefulness to the church is the same as significance to God. We'll tackle this last assumption right now.

Usefulness Is Not Significance

Usefulness is not the same as *significance*. Yes, within the context of the institutional church, a full-time minister is typically more useful to the body than a part-time volunteer. For example, it's generally best if our pastor stands up and preaches on Sunday morning, not our plumber. But let's not forget that it's generally best if our plumber shows up to fix our pipes on Thursday afternoon, not our pastor. Again, usefulness is not the same as significance. More specifically, you and I can't make ourselves significant to God by being useful to the church. God looks at the heart; therefore, a gift that is "higher" or more useful to the church does not make us "higher" or more significant to God.

If you have kids, then you can relate to this: my fourteen-year-old son is very useful around our house. He can cut firewood, shovel snow, and babysit his younger siblings. My five-year-old daughter, on the other hand, is adorable, but not exactly *useful.* Yet I'd lay down my life for either of them and their siblings, too. My children can never earn their significance to me; they are my sons and daughters. I love them all. I love them immeasurably. However, when it snows, I hand the shovel to my fourteen-year-old son, not my five-year-old daughter.

Jesus looked at the widow who gave two small copper coins—not exactly someone who was extremely useful to the church—and said, "Truly, I say to you, this poor widow has put in more than all those who are contributing to the offering box."[24] However, when Jesus launched his church, he gave the task of leadership to his highly gifted apostles—Peter, John, Paul, and the others—not the poor widow. A. W. Tozer said:

> Gifts differ within the body of Christ. A Billy Bray
> [nineteenth-century preacher who ministered to a
> small congregation in England] is not to be com-

---

[24] Mark 12:43

pared with a Luther or a Wesley for sheer usefulness to the church and to the world; but the service of the less gifted brother is as pure as that of the more gifted, and God accepts both with equal pleasure.[25]

Throughout church history, different gifts have surfaced as the "higher gifts"—the gifts that meet the church's primary need. Initially, the gift of apostleship was most important. At Pentecost, however, the gift of tongues was probably more important. Later, Paul said that the gift of prophecy was more important. Today, the gift of teaching seems to be the highest gift. But no matter which gift caries the banner, the Bible is clear: *usefulness* is not the same as *significance*. God is our Father—the giver of our gifts. Therefore, our significance is secure, and it has nothing to do with who has which gift.

God will build his church, and he will give us the gifts necessary for the task he sets before us. When the church sewage system backs up in the middle of a three-day ladies' conference, the highest gift in the body of Christ at that particular moment in history is plumbing, not preaching. "Now there are varieties of gifts, but the same Spirit; and there are varieties of service, but the same Lord; and there are varieties of activities, but it is the same God who empowers them all in everyone."[26] "For as in one body we have many members, and the members do not all have the same function, so we, though many, are one body in Christ, and individually members one of another."[27]

---

[25] Tozer, *The Pursuit of God,* 118.
[26] 1 Corinthians 12:4–6
[27] Romans 12:4–5

ONLY WHAT'S DONE FOR CHRIST WILL LAST

When we were little kids in Sunday school, our teacher, old Mrs. Johnson, taught us the poem, "Only one life, 'twill soon be past, Only what's done for Christ will last."

We all knew, of course, that Jesus didn't care one hoot about grown-up jobs like flying F-16 fighter jets, driving eighteen-wheelers, or being Spider-Man. Instead, Jesus wanted us to grow up and do "the Lord's work." According to Mrs. Johnson, that meant praying, witnessing, giving money to the church, or—most glorious of all—surrendering to the call of full-time Christian ministry. She told us that everything else we do in life will burn up in blazing flames and smoke when Jesus returns and annihilates the earth. She meant well, and she loved us like her own grand-children, but her definition of the Lord's work was incomplete. You and I should honor Mrs. Johnson, but we should turn to the Bible for the full definition of the Lord's work.

Without a doubt, the labor we traditionally define as "minis-try" is included in the biblical definition of the Lord's work. For example, the apostle Paul wrote to the Corinthian church and said, "Timothy . . . is doing the work of the Lord, as I am."[28] Timothy was a pastor, and Paul was an apostle. However, Paul clearly wasn't suggesting that the Corinthian believers should quit their jobs and become pastors or apostles. He was not implying that witnessing, preaching, and teaching are the only significant aspects of the Lord's work. Paul had already put that crazy notion to rest with his teaching about the body of Christ. Paul's view of the Lord's work

---

[28] 1 Corinthians 16:10

extended vastly beyond our narrowly defined list of ministry activities.

Paul described a particularly intriguing occupation as "for the Lord," "serving the Lord Christ." He used these exact words not to describe ministry work, but *slave* work. Slave work in those days meant everyday marketplace work and household toil. It meant building roads, managing estates, farming, accounting, cooking, running small businesses, scrubbing floors, and washing dishes. Paul admonished people to do these things "as for the Lord," "serving the Lord Christ." Many of the early New Testament church believers were slaves, doing much of the same work you and I do all week long.

> Slaves, obey in everything those who are your earthly masters, not by way of eye-service, as people-pleasers, but with sincerity of heart, fearing the Lord. Whatever you do, work heartily, as for the Lord and not for men, knowing that from the Lord you will receive the inheritance as your reward. You are serving the Lord Christ. (Colossians 3:22–24)

Slave work, done to the glory of God, is serving the Lord Christ; it is the work of the Lord. The Bible never justifies the tyranny of slavery. Instead, it subverts and defies the shackles of slavery. It gives us hope; not even the horror of slavery can rob our labor of its eternal significance.

Today, in the modern Western world, countless middle-class Christians feel like slaves. Talk to your friends; look around at the exhausted faces in church. Many of them feel like slaves to home mortgages, tough jobs, frenetic schedules, innumerable household chores—slaves to futility. But the Bible is clear: our "slave" labor is not futile; it's eternally significant. You and I should fight against slavery in all its forms;[29] meanwhile, we can take heart, because "from the Lord you will receive the inheritance as your reward."

Beyond slave work, the apostle Paul expanded the definition of the Lord's work to encompass *anything*. "Whatever you do, do all to the glory of God."[30] In case we'd be tempted to force-fit "whatever" into our preconceived notions of ministry, Paul gives us two paradigm-shattering examples of "whatever"—eating and drinking. Eating, drinking, slave work, preaching, teaching, whatever—do it all to the glory of God. You and I don't need to belabor the point any longer. Old Mrs. Johnson's definition of the Lord's work was incomplete.

In truth, Mrs. Johnson's life story is sad. She and thousands or perhaps millions just like her often heard the old-time preacher stomp and shout, "Only one life, 'twill soon be past, Only what's done for Christ will last." So naturally, near the end of their lives, they looked back at all they had done, and they despaired—*so little done for Christ; so little will last.* You see, Mrs. Johnson was a common laborer in a textile mill, which was little more than slave labor back in those days. Yet she believed that only her deeds of religious service mattered to Jesus; all else was vain. Her lament was this: aside from a few hours teaching Sunday school each week, "all else" was all she had.

Mrs. Johnson's story, however, has a spectacular ending. (Or perhaps it's just the beginning.) The moment she died and looked into her Creator's eyes, Mrs. Johnson—who throughout her life

---

[29] Isaiah 58:6–8, Proverbs 31:8–9, 1 Timothy 1:10, Philemon 16
[30] 1 Corinthians 10:31

radiated a beaming joy and love for Jesus—discovered an awesome surprise: her lifetime of labor and toil was not in vain after all; *it mattered to Jesus.* The old poem, it turns out, was true; but Mrs. Johnson had done far more for Christ than she ever imagined—far more that will last.

MARY, MARTHA, AND BUSY MOMS

Upon reading the story of Mary and Martha, countless homemakers and working moms feel horribly guilty, because they don't exactly "sit at the feet of Jesus" during a typical day of household chores. That guilt, however, is a lie.

> Jesus entered a village. And a woman named Martha welcomed him into her house. And she had a sister called Mary, who sat at the Lord's feet and listened to his teaching. But Martha was distracted with much serving. And she went up to him and said, "Lord, do you not care that my sister has left me to serve alone? Tell her then to help me." But the Lord answered her, "Martha, Martha, you are anxious and troubled about many things, but one thing is necessary. Mary has chosen the good portion, which will not be taken away from her." (Luke 10:38–42)

Long ago, monks used this passage to justify their lives of quiet solitude. Today, many Christians feel it teaches that the rat race of daily life is meaningless; only spiritual activities count for eternity. But John Calvin, the famed sixteenth-century reformer, thought otherwise. He blasted those who twisted the meaning of this passage.

> This passage has been basely distorted into the commendation of what is called a Contemplative life. . . . It is, no doubt, an old error, that those who withdraw from business, and devote themselves entirely to a contemplative [life], lead an Angelic life. For the absurdities which the [religious scholars] utter on this subject they appear to have been indebted to Aristotle. . . . On the contrary, we know that men were created for the express purpose of being employed in labour of various kinds, and that no sacrifice is more pleasing to God, than when every man applies diligently to his own calling. . . .

> Luke says that *Mary sat at the feet of Jesus.* Does he mean that she did nothing else throughout her whole life? On the contrary, the Lord enjoins his followers . . . there is a time to hear, and a time to act. It is, therefore, a foolish attempt of the monks to take hold of this passage, as if Christ were drawing a comparison between a contemplative life and an active life.[31]

Calvin went on to explain that Martha's action, though it was "right" and "deserved praise," was wrong because it was rooted in pride; it was all about Martha, not Jesus. Once again, the issue

---

[31] John Calvin, *Commentary on the Harmony of the Evangelists, Matthew, Mark, and Luke,* Vol. 2, trans. William Pringle (Edinburgh, Scotland: Calvin Translation Society, 1845), 142–143.

boils down to the heart, not the action. The action done in love "will not be taken away from her."[32] But "If I give away all I have, and if I deliver up my body to be burned, but have not love, I gain nothing."[33] "Martha was so delighted with her own bustling operations, as to despise her sister's pious eagerness to receive instruction. This example warns us, that, in doing what is right, we must take care not to think more highly of ourselves than others."[34]

Martha's labor was like that of a woman hosting Thanksgiving Day dinner—an act of loving service or even worship unless the hostess does it all for her own glory. Such a hostess spends the entire day bustling about and never sits down to enjoy a time of reflection and thanksgiving with her guests. She's so uptight and so intent on impressing everyone with her cooking that she despises the women who don't help her, thinking, *They're just sitting on their duffs.* In the end, her labor is really all about her own glory.

Biblical wisdom tells us there's a time to cook, and there's a time to sit down and listen.[35] When the Holy Son of the Most High God is teaching at your kitchen table, it's time to sit down and listen. However, God ordains that most (and sometimes *all*) of our time is rightly filled with cooking, cleaning, working, and trips to soccer practice. Sarah Edwards, wife of theologian Jonathan Edwards and mother of eleven children, said the daily toil of life, "attended with great alacrity, as part of the service of God" is "found to be as good as prayer."[36]

Calvin concludes, "There is no comparison here [between the contemplative and active], as unskillful and mistaken interpreters

---

[32] Luke 10:42
[33] 1 Corinthians 13:3
[34] Calvin, *Commentary on the Harmony of the Evangelists,* 144.
[35] Ecclesiastes 3:1–8
[36] Edwards, quoted in Piper, *Don't Waste Your Life,* 141.

dream."[37] If the Mary-Martha passage stood in complete isolation, then it would be possible to interpret it narrowly as a justification for legitimate vocational guilt. But this passage does not stand in isolation; it stands in the context of the entire Bible. The overwhelming weight of God's Word allows no such twisted distortion. In Calvin's words, using the Mary-Martha story to elevate ministry and contemplation over marketplace life or to heap guilt on busy moms is basely distorted, an old error, absurd, perverted, foolish, unskillful, and mistaken. (Sixteenth-century reformers were never big on subtlety or tact.)

Today's moms and homemakers still aren't convinced, however. Tripping over toys while lugging laundry down the stairs, day after day, somehow falls short of touching the eternal. Errand after errand, mess after mess, meal after meal—it's all temporal; their labor vanishes before their eyes. The likelihood that this work counts for eternity seems impossible. Worse, the daily grind of household chores does nothing useful for the church. Many moms feel guilty, because they don't have the time or energy to volunteer more hours at church—hours that impact souls and make a lasting difference.

I'll never forget when, after a particularly exhausting day, Misty looked at me and asked point-blank, "How exactly does washing a load of laundry change eternity?" So there it is—the question that must be answered. We long for our life's work to touch the eternal—to be part of something that lasts forever. But until we understand how washing a load of laundry (or writing a book, selling a motorcycle, designing a building, or operating a forklift) changes the shape of eternity, we will always feel that our

---

[37] Calvin, *Commentary on the Harmony of the Evangelists,* 144.

calling is a *lower* calling, our work is temporal, and what we do is meaningless in the grand scheme of things. The truth, however, is stunning. God uses our regular, daily, earthly work to forge the very shape of eternity. So let's turn the page and answer the question of how, exactly, this is true.

Chapter 10

Shaping an Unfinished Masterpiece

Behold! I tell you a mystery. . . . The dead will be
raised imperishable, and we shall be changed. For
this perishable body must put on the imperishable,
and this mortal body must put on immortality.

—1 Corinthians 15:51–53

Therefore, my beloved brothers, be steadfast, im-
movable, always abounding in the work of the
Lord, knowing that in the Lord your labor is not
in vain.

—1 Corinthians 15:58

I had always felt life first as a story: and if there is
a story there is a story-teller.

—G. K. Chesterton[1]

---

[1] G. K. Chesterton, *Orthodoxy* (Chicago: Moody, 2009), 93.

What is eternity? To understand how our everyday work forges the shape of eternity, we must first define eternity itself. For the sons and daughters of God, eternity is unending heaven. *But heaven is a nightmare*—at least, that's what many of us believe (and secretly fear). We imagine heaven to be an ethereal place where we strum golden harps, float on clouds, and sing in a choir forever and ever. Let's face it; that's a nightmare.

But that nightmare is not true. It's not the Bible's image of heaven. Our unappealing image of heaven is rooted in ancient Greek philosophic dualism, not the Bible. Remember, the Greeks postulated that the spiritual world is good, but the world of physical, earthy matter is somehow bad. They invented the divide between sacred and secular, higher and lower—the lie of the two-tier life. Consequently, you and I inherited a mystical image of heaven—a translucent world devoid of physical, earthly reality. But the Bible gives us a radically different image of heaven—an image that makes our hearts soar with eager anticipation, that makes us catch our breath and say, "Here at last is the thing I was made for."[2]

The Bible doesn't give us a crystal-clear, explicitly detailed description of heaven. It leaves many of the details to our imagination. However, the Bible fuels both our hope and our imagination

---

[2] Lewis, *The Problem of Pain,* 151.

with extraordinary images and thrilling hints about our future home. Based on these—and based on the biblically revealed truth of God's character, his creation, and his redemption of our lives—I believe that our eternal future is a physical future. It consists of real people with physical bodies interacting with a material universe. Heaven, after God's final victory over Satan, will not be a dreamy cloud bank. It will be, rather, redeemed creation—transformed and made new by God, "set free from its bondage to corruption."[3] The Bible describes heaven as a "new earth" set in the wonder of a new firmament (the "new heavens").[4] It will be a physical, material, real place; it will be the place where God once again walks with men and women. The marvel of it will buckle our knees and stagger our minds. Randy Alcorn, noted author and founder of Eternal Perspective Ministries, states:

> The predominant belief that the ultimate Heaven God prepares for us will be unearthly could not be more unbiblical. Earth was made for people to live on, and people were made to live on Earth. According to the prophets, the apostle Peter, and Christ himself, our destiny is to live forever on a restored and renewed Earth.[5]

Earth today, in its fallen state, is only a shadow of our eternal home—the new earth, the dwelling place of God with humankind. God will one day unite heaven and earth under his reign. He will redeem his material creation, transform it, and make it new in its perfect, physical state. You and I will behold it in awe, and like

---

[3] Romans 8:21
[4] Isaiah 65:17, 66:22; 2 Peter 3:13; Revelation 21:1
[5] Alcorn, *Heaven,* 92.

the characters of Narnia, exclaim, "I have come home at last! This is my real county! I belong here. This is the land I have been looking for all my life."[6] In his meditation on prayer, C. S. Lewis writes, "The hills and valleys of Heaven will be to those you now experience not as a copy is to an original, nor as a substitute is to the genuine article, but as the flower to the root, or the diamond to the coal."[7]

An acorn must first pass away before it is raised up as a giant oak tree. Similarly, the earth will pass away before God raises it up as the new earth. And as the oak tree is massively more spectacular than the acorn, so the new earth will also surpass the curse-bound earth we see today. At the end of this age, the holy fire of God's judgment will dissolve the universe and lay the earth bare. The earth will pass away.[8] But then God will redeem the earth and make it new. He will transform it. The diamond will emerge from the coal.

"Not the mere immortality of the soul, but rather the resurrection of the body and the renewal of all creation is the hope of the Christian faith,"[9] writes John Piper. Later he continues, "God's curse on the creation in Genesis 3 is not his final word. He did it 'in hope.' Therefore creation is not appointed for annihilation, but for restoration."[10] Romans 8:18–24 shows us the hope-filled promise of creation's future redemption. Here God links creation's redemption to our future redemption as the sons and daughters of God:

---

[6] C. S. Lewis, *The Last Battle* (New York: HarperCollins, 1994), 196.

[7] C. S. Lewis, *Letters to Malcolm: Chiefly on Prayer* (San Diego: Harcourt, 2002), 123.

[8] 2 Peter 3:10–13

[9] John Piper, *Future Grace: The Purifying Power of Living by Faith in Future Grace* (New York: Multnomah, 1995), 374.

[10] Piper, *Future Grace,* 377.

For I consider that the sufferings of this present time are not worth comparing with the glory that is to be revealed to us. For the creation waits with eager longing for the revealing of the sons of God. For the creation was subjected to futility, not willingly, but because of him who subjected it, in hope that the creation itself will be set free from its bondage to corruption and obtain the freedom of the glory of the children of God. For we know that the whole creation has been groaning together in the pains of childbirth until now. And not only the creation, but we ourselves, who have the firstfruits of the Spirit, groan inwardly as we wait eagerly for adoption as sons, the redemption of our bodies. For in this hope we were saved. (Romans 8:18–24)

God will unleash creation from the chains of the curse—chains against which it fiercely strains, longing to "obtain the freedom of the glory of the children of God."[11] Then creation, like an unfettered stallion, will burst forth in determined, wild freedom—an ever-expanding, astonishing display of God's power, wisdom, and glory. All the hosts of heaven will wonder at the sight of it, for this will also be their home,[12] the dwelling place of humans, angels, and God. This is the new heaven and earth—his glorious masterpiece.

---

[11] Romans 8:21
[12] 1 Corinthians 6:3, Hebrews 12:22–23

Throughout the remainder of this chapter, we will explore three ways our everyday labor, in the Master's grip, makes a lasting difference in heaven—in other words, three ways it forges the shape of eternity. First, our labor shapes human lives. It shapes us, and it shapes other people, too. Our lives have no ending; they'll be present on the new earth forever. Second, the labor we do today determines the rewards we will enjoy and steward on the new earth for all eternity. Third, in some form, if done to the glory of God, our labor will be carried forward into the new earth. God will resurrect, redeem, and transform our labor, as strange as it sounds, and integrate it into the reality of heaven. Randy Alcorn put it this way: "Just as we will be carried over from the old world to the new, so will our labor."[13]

EVERLASTING PEOPLE

Our lives—our stories—have no ending. Your labors, interests, experiences, skills, relationships, trials, victories, and defeats forge who you are; all of it will be part of you forever. You are everlasting. It's you—the real you—who will be resurrected to eternal life, not some nameless, faceless, boring wraith. God will not erase your memory, personality, and life history when he returns. Instead, he will redeem and transform every aspect of your life. Good or bad, spectacular or mundane—all of it will be healed from the wounds of sin. You will be you for all eternity. C. S. Lewis writes, "All that you are, sins apart, is destined, if you will let God have His good way, to utter satisfaction."[14]

---

[13] Alcorn, *Heaven*, 133.
[14] Lewis, *The Problem of Pain*, 152.

Every second of our lives, every experience, and every labor (small or great) shapes who we are and who we will always be. Misty, who washed 4,376 loads of laundry, will one day be resurrected to everlasting life in heaven. You, who are reading these words this very instant and did whatever else you did today, will be resurrected. Moses, who tended sheep for forty years in the wilderness, will tell us stories about the burning bush. Through our unique, God-given vocations today, God prepares us for our eternal vocations—our own unique capacity to reflect his glory forever.

Our labor shapes other lives, too. Think of the people you work with each day. You shape who they are and who they will be for all eternity. Misty's labor, as Senior Chief Executive Director of our household, profoundly shapes my life. Since you are reading these words, her labor shapes your life, too. Though the imprint is slight, a faint brushstroke on a lifelong canvas, it is everlasting; the masterpiece of eternity would not be complete without it. Whether you're a popular Christian music star singing to thirty thousand swaying fans or an exhausted mom singing to a fussy baby at 2:00 a.m., you shape immortal lives.

You are absolutely unique, forged by a lifetime of God-authored experiences. The shape of you reflects a unique aspect of God's glory—an aspect that only you, and forever only you, can reflect. That's why he made you; that's the whole point of your uniqueness. "Man's chief end is to glorify God, and to enjoy him forever."[15] The point of being you will not change when you get to heaven. "Each of the redeemed shall forever know and praise some one aspect of the Divine beauty better than any other creature,"

---

[15] *Westminster Shorter Catechism*, in Orthodox Presbyterian Church, *The Westminster Confession of Faith and Catechisms*, 355.

writes Lewis, who added that if we all "returned [God] an identical worship, the song of the Church triumphant would have no symphony, it would be like an orchestra in which all the instruments played the same note."[16]

There's a divine story that only you can tell, because God has given you a life like no one else's. The marvel of it—the breathtaking wonder of what God is forging you to be—will blaze forth so that redeemed humankind and all the hosts of heaven will forever behold the splendor of it. Only you, a unique son or daughter of God, can reveal your particular aspect of his glory to the rest of us. That's why you have a story to tell us, an amazing story—and that story is you, an everlasting, dazzling facet of God's infinite perfection.

ETERNAL REWARDS

Because you paved a road, washed a load of laundry, or met with a client today, eternity will be different. It will be different not only because your labor shaped everlasting lives, but also because God promises eternal rewards for your labor. This is staggering: because of our labor today, God will create a treasure—a reward of unutterable beauty—that will be part of the new earth and reflect his glory forever.

God's promise of eternal rewards is meant to encourage our hearts and bolster our strength. But for many of us, it causes more discouragement (vocational guilt) than encouragement. The trouble is that we assume God only rewards *sacred* labor, which of

---

[16] Lewis, *The Problem of Pain*, 154–155.

course, we've defined as acts of religious service or ministry. But our assumption is wrong. God promises rewards for acts of ministry, but he also promises rewards for our marketplace toil.

Ephesians 6:8 is one of the great rewards passages in the Bible: "The Lord will reward everyone for whatever good he does."[17] This passage doesn't promise rewards for acts of religious service. Instead, it promises eternal rewards for the everyday labor and household tasks of bondservants and masters.[18] Today, you and I would simply call them employees and bosses.

There is, however, a condition attached to the promise: God only rewards labor that is done "wholeheartedly, as if you were serving the Lord, not men."[19] This is another way of saying that God only rewards labor that is done to the glory of God, not the glory of self. The condition is absolute; it applies equally to all labor, whether it's business, ministry, or household chores. Remember, Jesus blasted ministry workers who did their religious deeds for their own glory. The problem wasn't their work; it was their heart. Jesus said, "Beware of practicing your righteousness before other people in order to be seen by them, for then you will have no reward from your Father who is in heaven."[20] But he also said we *will* receive an eternal reward for our labor—whether it's building a cabinet or preaching a sermon—*if* it's done to the glory of God, not self.

When Misty and I were in Egypt, we saw the fabulous treasures of the ancient pharaohs. Those guys thought they could take their wealth with them to heaven, so they amassed tons of gold and stacked it in their tombs. Their goal was to make themselves

---

[17] Ephesians 6:8 (NIV)
[18] Ephesians 6:5–9, Colossians 3:22–4:1
[19] Ephesians 6:7 (NIV), Colossians 3:22–25
[20] Matthew 6:1

glorious both in the present life and in the next. But they got it all backwards. Wealth that is given away and labor done to the glory of God build up treasures in heaven. If one of those pharaohs is in heaven today, then he's a peasant by new earth standards. By contrast, the poor widow, who gave away her last two copper coins—the world has not yet seen the likes of her royal wealth and beauty . . . and authority.

The Bible describes eternal rewards not only as treasures, but also as positions of authority. It speaks of our ruling over cities, judging angels, wearing crowns, and reigning with Christ. The master said to his servant, "Well done, good and faithful servant. You have been faithful over a little; I will set you over much."[21] The significance of our labor today is staggering, because in this vapor of time we call life, you and I determine our capacity to reign over the new earth as "heirs of God and fellow heirs with Christ."[22] We forge, in part, the shape of our everlasting vocations—what we'll do forever.

"God is most glorified in us," John Piper writes, "when we are most satisfied in him."[23] In other words, we fulfill our chief end—we glorify God—*by* enjoying God. Thus we begin to see the true wonder of our eternal rewards. Whether treasures or positions of authority, these rewards will reveal particular aspects of God's glory to us. They will give us higher capacities to uniquely see and enjoy the glory of God for all eternity.

God's glory is our greatest joy. It's what we're made for. It's the deep longing of our hearts. Our ache for significance will only be satisfied when we dwell with him in perfect unity with his Son.

---

[21] Matthew 25:21
[22] Romans 8:17
[23] Piper, *Desiring God*, 50.

There our rewards will magnify his breathtaking perfection and open to us vast expanses of his glory—vast expanses of our joy. Our fathomless delight will not be found in the rewards themselves but in the one they reveal—the source of all glory. Yes, our rewards will be unspeakably beautiful, but we will look straight through them and right into the eyes of the master craftsman, the Creator of them all. Our joy will be utterly complete forever.

LABOR'S MIND-BENDING DESTINY

The Bible seems to indicate that if our labor is done to the glory of God, then in some form, the labor itself will be redeemed and resurrected into heaven.

To me, this immediately sounds bizarre—severely bizarre. It probably sounds that way to you, too. A resurrected spreadsheet? What about the labor of refereeing a high school hockey game, washing a load of laundry, or teaching? This image is flat-out mind-bending. Consequently, theologians who write about it almost always use examples of labor that produces tangible products like chairs and paintings. You and I can imagine a chair and a painting in heaven, but getting our minds around a resurrected spreadsheet is just too far out there (and frankly, too terrifying). But in Western societies, many of us earn our daily bread by producing things like spreadsheets, lesson plans, and clean loads of laundry, not tangible products like chairs and paintings.

Our hope for our labor's eternal impact does not hinge on this nearly incomprehensible image of resurrected deeds. It's not the linchpin. It is, however, an image held out to us from the pages of the Bible, though only faintly. The Bible doesn't make it explicitly clear, but the very possibility that our work could somehow be transformed into a spectacular, God-glorifying eternal reality overwhelms us with the wonder of God's power and love. And that, I believe, is precisely why God gave us this truth. So let's take it up for a few paragraphs, and let's worship him.

Randy Alcorn, in his comprehensive book on heaven, writes, "God promises to resurrect not only humanity but also the creation that fell as a result of our sin. Because God will resurrect the earth itself, we know that the resurrection of the dead extends to things that are inanimate. Even some of the works of our hands, done to God's glory, will survive. . . . Scripture is clear that in some form, at least, what's done on Earth to Christ's glory will survive."[24]

In 1 Corinthians 3:13–14, the apostle Paul linked together three distinct concepts: God's purifying fire, works that survive, and eternal rewards. "Paul appears to be saying more than just that we will be rewarded for what we did on Earth," Alcorn observes. "He appears to be saying that what we did on Earth will itself endure."[25] Paul wrote, "Each one's work will become manifest, for the Day will disclose it, because it will be revealed by fire, and the fire will test what sort of work each one has done. If the work that anyone has built on the foundation survives, he will receive a reward."[26]

---

[24] Alcorn, *Heaven,* 135–136.
[25] Alcorn, *Heaven,* 134.
[26] 1 Corinthians 3:13–14

Revelation 14:13 says, "'Blessed are the dead who die in the Lord from now on.' 'Blessed indeed,' says the Spirit, 'that they may rest from their labors, for their deeds follow them!'" In Revelation 19:7–8, we read, "'The marriage of the Lamb has come, and his Bride [the resurrected church] has made herself ready; it was granted to her to clothe herself with fine linen, bright and pure'— for the fine linen is the righteous deeds of the saints." And according to the Bible, righteous deeds include everyday work done to the glory of God. How exactly the church can be clothed with deeds is totally beyond me, but God, the author, seems to purposely emphasize that in some form, our deeds will be there, and they'll be stunning.

The Bible says God will "reconcile to himself all things, whether on earth or in heaven, making peace by the blood of his cross."[27] All things means *all things*.[28] God aims to be eternally glorified by everything, small or great, that has taken place since the dawn of creation, and that includes the works of our hands.

God doesn't spell out the details. What does it mean for our deeds to survive, follow us, and be reconciled to him? The biblical images of resurrected deeds are faint and unclear. We simply can't be certain what they will be. We can, however, be absolutely certain that God gives us eternal hope for our labor—a resurrection hope. As to the details, he says, "I am God, the Creator of the universe. Trust me with your labor and toil." So we look toward heaven, and we pray:

---

[27] Colossians 1:20

[28] However, "all things" does *not* imply universalism or the universal salvation of all people. Those who reject God "will go away into eternal punishment," not reconciliation. Hell is real, and it is eternal. See Matthew 8:12, 13:49–50, 25:46; 2 Thessalonians 1:9; and Revelation 14:11.

The years of our life are seventy,
or even by reason of strength eighty;
yet their span is but toil and trouble. . . .
Return, O Lord! How Long?
Have pity on your servants! . . .
Let the favor of the Lord our God be upon us,
and establish the work of our hands upon us;
yes, establish the work of our hands!
(Psalm 90:10, 13, 17)

At a fundamental level, the distinctions are unimportant. Whether through transformed deeds, eternal rewards, or everlasting lives shaped by our labor, one thing is sure: your labor, done to the glory of God, makes a lasting difference in eternity. There is a direct link between the labor you do today and the future reality of heaven. God designed eternity, his masterpiece, with your fingerprints all over it.

AN ANALOGY TO THE RESURRECTION FULFILLMENT OF OUR LIVES

Limited by human reasoning, it's tough for us to fathom how God will physically resurrect and transform our lives. How exactly will a mortal body be "raised imperishable"[29] —even a body that died and vanished long ago? And what about the possibility of resurrected and transformed acts of labor? Many people simply don't worry about it. They trust God at his Word and move on with life.

---

[29] 1 Corinthians 15:52–54

They're the smart ones. But the rest of us, including me, can't help but ponder the scientific quandaries of our future resurrection. I offer the following analogy to help move us past those quandaries. If you're one of the smart ones, skip it. It's not doctrine; it's purely my musing, though it does contain a true story and some intriguing facts.

—————— ∞∞∞ ——————

"Unbuilt." The word was never meant to be there, but it was stamped beneath a Frank Lloyd Wright architectural plan for a masterpiece that was never built. In the late 1920s, Wright designed an innovative glass skyscraper to be located at 2nd Avenue and 11th street in New York City. It would have been a marvel. But the Great Depression hit the country, and the skyscraper never became a reality.

Wright's part of the work, however, was complete: he had created the design. Frank Lloyd Wright was an architect, not a builder. An architect's task is essentially to create a vision—a mental image of a possible building. The stack of pencil sketches and plans Wright created were the means of conveying his work (his vision) to the builder. The sketches and plans themselves were not the finished product, just as black marks on a page are not the finished product of a songwriter. Hence, just as every songwriter deeply yearns to hear his song sung by a great musician, every architect yearns for a master builder to take up his vision and transform it into a physical reality.

Wright's work on this project went no further than a vision. His labor appears to have been utterly meaningless, because nobody with sufficient power and wealth carried the project forward to its ultimate glory. It simply died, and that was the end of it. However, nearly a hundred years later, you and I could quite literally resurrect Frank Lloyd Wright's glass skyscraper vision.

In a sense, Wright's work would have vanished from the universe altogether if not for one critical fact: it is recorded in those pencil sketches and plans. Because it is recorded, it exists. Therefore, you and I can *resurrect* it—we can study those sketches and plans, and we can visualize the precise image he created. Beyond that, we can *transform* it—with the help of a powerful master builder, we can build it. We can make Wright's vision of a glass skyscraper into a physical reality, the marvel it was always meant to be. The unbuilt work, though only a vision and a sketch, would be gloriously resurrected and transformed. The unbuilt would be built.

Today, no matter who we are and no matter what our work is—whether we fly helicopters, scrub toilets, manage stock portfolios, or cook pizzas—our lives and labor would eventually vanish from the universe altogether if not for one critical fact: they are recorded in the infinite knowledge of God, the ultimate reality. Because they are recorded, they exist. They exist forever. In their glorified form, apart from sin, our lives and labor will be part of eternity.

But how will our Savior resurrect and transform bodies that have vanished? What about the nearly incomprehensible possibility of transformed labor, especially intangible labor—flying a helicopter, scrubbing a toilet, or managing a stock portfolio? Again, the Bible simply doesn't tell us—at least, not explicitly. But consider this: God is God. He created the entire universe, including over 200 billion galaxies, out of absolutely nothing.

Every life and every act of labor, tangible or not, whether it took place two seconds ago or two thousand years ago, is an absolute reality in the ever-present knowledge of God. The life happened. The act happened. It was a real, historic, space-time event in the universe, and now it is held in the mind of God, the source of all that exists. God, who spoke the universe into existence out of nothing, is entirely capable of creating a breathtaking wonder out of our lives and labor—even our labor of updating a spreadsheet or washing a load of laundry. His infinite wisdom and power transcend the nuances, though incomprehensible to our minds, of intangible labor, vanishing lives, and scattered atomic particles. "For by him all things were created, in heaven and on earth, visible and invisible . . . all things were created through him and for him. And he is before all things, and in him all things hold together."[30]

The realities we know today—the earth, our labor, our bodies, our lives—are all mere shadows of what they will one day be. They are unbuilt. It's like comparing an architect's pencil sketch to an actual skyscraper made of glass and steel. What the shadow needs in order to become real is the master builder—the one who has the power to carry the project forward to its ultimate glory. Today we battle against sin, death, and decay. Our lives and labor appear to be utterly meaningless. We die, and that seems to be the end of it. The day is coming, however, when God will gather up our labor, our lives, and creation. He will transform each into the marvel it was always meant to be. Our Lord and Creator, the master builder, will transform the shadow into a breathtaking reality. He will sing the unsung song. He will build the unbuilt masterpiece.

---

[30] Colossians 1:16–17

THE WORK OF HIS HANDS

"Look what Daddy did! Look what Daddy did! Look . . ." yelled my six-year-old son as he ran through the house with a huge smile on his face. He held up a piece of paper, rumpled and thoroughly smudged, for everyone else in the family to see. Daddy had done a miracle.

I was working in my study when he walked in and handed me a pencil drawing. "Daddy, I drew you a picture."

I beamed, "Oh, wow. That is *sooo* amazing—you drew a car, and next to it you drew . . . um, ah, a circle?"

"No, Daddy, it's a bouncy ball." Apparently, the car was about to crash into a giant bouncy ball, which is precisely what cars are supposed to do when you're six.

I asked my son, "Would you like me to make your picture look more real?" His head nodded vigorously in the affirmative. Then he sat and watched in wide-eyed wonder as I added 3-dimensional perspective lines, shadows, and shading. His simple line drawing came to life. The circle became a ball, bouncing in midair. The car, once flat and still, raced across the paper.

My son carried that picture around for weeks, showing it to nearly everyone he met. He wanted the whole world to see the wonder of it. "Look what Daddy did!" The thing that struck me most, apart from my delight in his vibrant joy, was that my son never said, "Look what *I* did! Look what *I* did!" He always said, "Look what *Daddy* did!" The original picture, after all, was the work of his little hands—simple and childish, but his nonetheless. Yet now that it was transformed into a "masterpiece," he ran around, giving Daddy all the glory.

I suspect that one day, you and I will do the same thing. When we behold the wonder that God has made of the earth, our labor, and our lives, we will run around in heaven, pointing and yelling, "Look what Daddy did! Look what Daddy did!" The overwhelming magnitude of the transformation will attest to the power and glory of God, not us. In the presence of his manifest glory, human pride will be inconceivable. Yes, we lived our lives, and we labored. We drew God a simple, childish picture. But the marvel he will make of it, the masterpiece, is the work of his hands, not ours. Never again will the words "Look what *I* did" cross our lips.

The extent and the wonder of our coming transformation are unfathomable; it is outside human experience and vastly beyond our comprehension. But the Bible gives us breathtaking glimmers. The Bible says there exists today a prototype of our future, resurrected bodies: his name is Jesus. Our bodies will be resurrected and transformed "to be like his glorious body."[31] His glorious body isn't just a spirit; it is also flesh and bones.[32] Our bodies, not just our souls, will become immortal. Yet Jesus' body is not *merely* resurrected flesh and bones; it is more. Much more! After his resurrection, Jesus had a real, flesh and bones, physical body that could vanish into thin air, walk through walls, and ascend into heaven. His was a physical body with unimaginable powers. The architect's pencil sketch became a skyscraper.

The Corinthian church asked the apostle Paul, "How are the dead raised? With what kind of body do they come?" He replied, "What you sow does not come to life unless it dies. And what you sow is not the body that is to be, but a bare kernel, perhaps of wheat or of some other grain. But God gives it a body as he has

---

[31] Philippians 3:21
[32] Luke 24:39–43

237

chosen, and to each kind of seed its own body."[33] The bare kernel is resurrected to become a wheat plant that is hundreds of times larger and phenomenally more complex. Just think of it—our bodies, in some way, will be hundreds of times more capable of experiencing and enjoying the glory of God. Our chief end remains forever unchanged, but our capacity to fulfill our chief end will increase phenomenally.

We will need those transformed bodies, because the new earth is more than today's earth—much more! The Bible says the new Jerusalem[34]—the capital city of the new earth—is built of jasper and pure gold. Its length and width are the same—1,400 miles, the distance between Winnipeg, Canada and San Carlos, Mexico. The real shocker is that the city is 1,400 miles *high*. The Empire State Building is a quarter-mile high, passenger jets fly seven miles above the earth's surface, and spacecraft orbit the earth at an altitude of three hundred miles. If the new Jerusalem were on earth today, satellites would slam into its walls. It's unclear whether the measurements given by the Bible are literal or figurative, but the point of the Bible's vivid description is absolutely clear: The earth will be transformed. It will be incomprehensibly more spectacular than it is today; it will be the dwelling place of God and humankind.

The vastness and unutterable beauty of the new earth staggers the imagination. Yet because we update spreadsheets, vacuum floors, and repair power steering pumps to God's glory, he creates treasures that will be part of this wonder. He uses our work to shape lives that will be there forever. Our deeds will follow us. He will transform our lives to be everlasting reflections of his glory.

---

[33] 1 Corinthians 15:35–38
[34] Revelation 21:10–18

Dare we hope? How can we possibly believe that our labor and vocations—our random-arrow lives—will in some unfathomable way make a lasting difference in eternity? The leap seems too far until we remember that God is not only our sovereign Master, but also our Father, who delights in the adoration and joy of his sons and daughters. He takes up our simple, childish labors, our vocations—our lives—and makes them his masterpiece, the work of his hands, not ours.

Over the years, my kids have given me hundreds of rumpled and smudged pieces of art. An entire wall of my office is now covered in crayon pictures, pencil drawings, and finger paintings. A few months ago, while leaning back in my chair and staring at my wall of treasures, I pondered to myself, *If I were God, Creator of the universe, what would I do with these little gifts of love?* My eyes suddenly froze on a single finger painting high up on the wall. One of my daughters had finger-painted a paper plate, presumably after eating her sandwich off of it, with vibrant swirls of color pinwheeling out from the center. The idea struck me, and I gasped: to my fatherly eyes, that simple, childish, finger-painted paper plate looked just like a galaxy.

I'd make it real; that's what I would do. If I were God, I'd take up that little work of my daughter's hands, and I'd touch it with the infinite power of my glory. I'd transform it into a cosmic wonder—a physical reality, an actual galaxy. And oh, what a wonder it would be. Sentimental and sappy? Yes, but daddies tend to be that way when it comes to their kids. Anyone else would look at her labor, just blobs of paint smeared on a paper plate, and think it's useless—utterly insignificant in the grand scheme of things. But I'm her daddy. I see things differently.

When you and I were born, God handed us the crayons, pencils, and finger paints of life. Then our loving Father smiled and said, "Go ahead, live the life I gave you to live. Paint a picture for me." So we live our random-arrow lives. We labor, nine rows back, third from the left. With stubby little hands, we smear blobs of paint on the paper-plate canvas of life. In the end, God—the great I AM, the Almighty—will tenderly take up our lives and labor. He will beam, "Oh, wow. That is so amazing. You painted, um, ah, a . . ." Then he will touch our efforts with the infinite power of his glory—and what astonishing, breathtaking wonders they will be.

Our unseen toil, our unnoticed talents, our unapplauded lives—God will make them each a marvel. What exactly will they look like? We can only imagine. This, however, is sure: he will make them more spectacular than we ever dreamed they could be. They'll be part of his masterpiece, displayed on the canvas of eternity. He will do all of this so that for all the coming ages, you and I and all the hosts of heaven will behold the wonder of it and cry out, "Look! Look what Daddy did! Look what Daddy did!"

CHAPTER 11

THE BEGINNING OF OUR EVERLASTING VOCATIONS

You have had your say. Others may have had their say. But make no judgments and draw no conclusions until the scaffolding of history is stripped away and you see what it means for God to have had his say—and made you what you are called to be.

—Os Guinness[1]

I glorified you on earth, having accomplished the work that you gave me to do. And now, Father, glorify me in your own presence.

—Jesus[2]

The dream is ended: this is the morning.

—C. S. Lewis[3]

---

[1] Os Guinness, *The Call*, 232.
[2] John 17:4–5
[3] Lewis, *The Last Battle*, 210.

The year was 1517. Insulting the church—a world political power dominated by the religious elite—could lead to your being burned to death at the stake. But a daring wild-man jumped onto history's center stage. Aided by the modern marvel of the printing press, he hurled unprecedented insults at the church establishment. His name was Martin Luther. Incensed by the church's abuse of power, Luther—an all-in-one brilliant scholar, caring pastor, and vociferous agitator—famously posted his Ninety-Five Theses and ignited a global firestorm: the Reformation.

Today, Luther is well-known for his role in the Reformation, but few of us are aware that he was a fierce champion and defender of everyday marketplace vocations. "It is pure invention," he wrote, "that pope, bishops, priests and monks [the clergy of his day] are to be called the 'spiritual estate'; princes, lords, artisans, and farmers the 'temporal estate.' That is indeed a fine bit of lying and hypocrisy."[4] Luther unleashed particularly livid blasts on anyone who claimed a person could earn a higher standing with God by abandoning their "temporal" or "secular" vocations and cloistering themselves away in full-time church work. He said, "They are a perverted people that perverts all the laws of God. . . . Yet they hope for higher thrones in heaven than common Christians will

---

[4] Martin Luther, "An Open Letter to the Christian Nobility of the German Nation Concerning the Reform of the Christian Estate," In *Callings: Twenty Centuries of Christian Wisdom on Vocation*, edited by William C. Placher (Grand Rapids: William B. Eerdmans, 2005), 211.

receive. No, in the abyss of hell they will sit, they who pervert heavenly freedom into such an infernal prison."[5]

Luther rocked the world with a message that, in spite of its being drawn from the pages of the Bible, was considered heretical by the ministry professionals of his day. Luther declared that the epic battle of the universe was being fought not in the opulent church buildings of sixteenth century Europe but in the context of everyday, grueling peasant toil. This flew in the face of the organized church, which claimed that only those in the ministry had a true vocation, a higher call, an eternally significant life. Five hundred years later, I sit and listen to sermons, testimonies, conference presentations, and interviews with wildly popular Christian music stars, and I quietly wonder, *Has anything really changed?*

It's important to remember that Luther loved the church. He was a preacher, and he encouraged others who were skilled for the task to enter the ministry. Luther's incendiary pen was never aimed categorically at the church or those who served in the offices of pastor, monk, or priest. Rather, it was aimed (with great intensity) at the hearts of those who, by virtue of being in the ministry or performing religious deeds, felt they were somehow more valuable to God than people with marketplace vocations. To that end, he wrote, "The works of monks and priests, however holy and arduous they may be, do not differ one whit in the sight of God from the works of the rustic laborer in the field or the woman going about her household tasks, but that all works are measured before God by faith alone."[6]

---

[5] Luther, quoted in Wingren, *Luther on Vocation,* 101.
[6] Martin Luther, "The Babylonian Captivity of the Church," in *Three Treatises,* trans. and rev. A. T. W. Steinhäuser, et al. (Philadelphia: Fortress Press, 1970), 202–203.

Luther was not alone in his fierce opposition to the lie of the sacred-secular divide—the lie of vocational guilt. "There is no work better than another to please God," said William Tyndale, Luther's English contemporary. "To pour water, to wash dishes, to be a souter [cobbler], or an apostle, all is one, to wash dishes and to preach is all one, as touching the deed, to please God."[7]

Why would these theologians, famous for their daring roles in the Reformation, champion everyday vocations? What drove Tyndale, Luther, and others like them to such ardent defense of "the works of the rustic laborer in the field or the woman going about her household tasks"? The answer lies at the heart of the Reformation—the rediscovery of the gospel. Eternal salvation (and thereby eternal significance to God) is by grace alone through faith. It is a gift from God that was purchased with the blood of his Son, Jesus Christ. Nothing we do, not even full-time ministry work, can earn us one single atom of favor with God Almighty. We bring absolutely nothing to the table, but we get everything.

The medieval church, having slipped its Biblical moorings, lost sight of the priceless wonder of the gospel. And the freedom of faith became the infernal prison of self-justification. Blinded by pride, the church anchored people's eternal significance in their own works and merit—what they could accomplish, discover, attain, and prove. The church stated that people earned their place in eternity and could determine their level of everlasting worth. But the horror of self-justification closes in on us the moment we realize our plight. If our eternal worth depends on what we do, then we can never do enough. The weight of eternity is cosmic; we are but worm food—hopeless.

---

[7] Tyndale, quoted in Paul R. Stevens, *Doing God's Business: Meaning and Motivation for the Marketplace* (Grand Rapids: William B. Eerdmans, 2006), 222.

Luther and his fellow reformers, seeing the fatal trap lurking in this church-sanctioned abomination, shouted to the world, "No! It is a lie. Self-justification is a lie from the pit of hell. Salvation is by grace alone through faith; it is a gift to be received, not earned." They called for a return to the gospel; they restored the hope of eternal significance to the miller, cobbler, baker, craftsman, and rustic laborer in the field; they risked their lives to proclaim the truth; and they turned the world upside down. What drove them? The life-giving, ultimate freedom of the gospel.

THE FINISHED WORK OF JESUS CHRIST

Against the horror of earning our own eternal significance, against the belief that we can become more important *to* God by doing something *for* God, and against the paradigm that says assistant pastors are more valuable to God than truck drivers—against all this stands the echoing thunderclap of eternity: "It is finished."[8] Those three words, the final cry of Jesus on the cross, irrevocably declare our eternal significance and seal it in holy blood. Any attempt to earn or prove our worth to God is an outright desecration of the gospel; it's an attempt to circumvent the life, death, and resurrection of Jesus Christ. Jesus said, "I am the way, and the truth, and the life. No one comes to the Father except through me."[9] He paid our ransom. There is nothing we can do to add to it or somehow improve upon his effort. It is finished.

The gospel frees us to live our random-arrow lives with all our might, with hope, and *without* guilt. We have nothing to prove to

---

[8] John 19:30
[9] John 14:6

God; the finished work of Jesus is all the proof God needs. Our task is to present our lives as living sacrifices to him—lives of worship that are lived in awe of what he did.[10]

Having been freed by the gospel from the bondage of justifying our worth, we follow our mighty captain into the heart of the battle. There we fulfill our God-given duties. We design, sell, build, trade, manage, negotiate, and write. We wash loads and loads of laundry. God is the author who guides our lives into the unique spheres of our vocations—our work, roles, and relationships—our little slivers of the all in all. He doesn't ask us to conquer the world single-handedly on his behalf. Rather, he says, "Whatever your hand finds to do, do it with all your might, do it all for the glory of God"[11]—and that includes driving a truck.

The struggle against vocational guilt is ultimately a struggle to lay hold of—to live, breathe, trust, know, and utterly experience—the life-giving freedom of the gospel. The degree to which you and I experience vocational freedom, apart from sin, is the degree to which you and I believe the cry of Jesus: "It is finished." The gospel anchors our hope, significance, and worth in the infinitely worthy Son of God. As such, our value to God infinitely transcends our labor and the circumstances of our lives. Jesus Christ is the living embodiment of our hope, significance, and worth. He has just one question for you and me. It's the question of our eternal destiny: "Do you trust me?"

Jesus leads us into the battle. He sweeps us up into his story—the epic of eternity, his masterpiece. The lie of vocational guilt whispers, "What you do determines your significance," but the Lord God of heaven and earth thunders, "What My Son did on

---

[10] Romans 12:1
[11] Ecclesiastes 9:10 (NIV), 1 Corinthians 10:31 (NIV)

the cross determines your significance!" Our significance is secure, infinitely unshakable, and eternal. We will forever reign over the new earth as heirs of God and fellow heirs with Christ[12] —but not all of us. For we are not all sons and daughters of God.

THE UNBELIEVER'S LABOR AND SUMMONS

Unbelievers—people who reject the gospel of Jesus Christ—shape eternity, too. Their lives, vocations, and toil participate in God's providential care of humankind and creation, and all of it shapes everlasting lives. Think of all the people who have influenced your life—the people who have made you who you are. Also consider the vast, globe-spanning network of people who make your life possible each day. By 9:00 a.m. each day, we have put on clothing, used technology, and eaten food, all of which was shipped to us from the four corners of world. Many, if not most, of those people are unbelievers. They forge the shape of eternity—but not their own eternity.

Unbelievers will not see eternity. They'll never see the wonder of the new earth. They'll never know the fathomless joy of dwelling there with God. They won't experience eternal life. They will experience, rather, eternal horror. For in rejecting Jesus Christ, they choose hell.

No amount of good works—not even a life dedicated to feeding the world's hungry—can merit everlasting life in heaven. That "narrow-minded" statement angers many people today, but the Bible is decisively clear on this. "For by grace you have been saved through faith. And this is not your own doing; it is the gift of

---

[12] Romans 8:17

247

God, not a result of works, so that no one may boast."[13] "He saved us, not because of works done by us in righteousness, but according to his own mercy."[14]

God's mercy is the gospel—the life, death, and resurrection of Jesus Christ. Those who deny his mercy deny the risen Son. The Bible says, "If we deny him, he also will deny us."[15] Whomever he denies "will suffer the punishment of eternal destruction, away from the presence of the Lord and from the glory of his might."[16] The angels will "throw them into the fiery furnace. In that place there will be weeping and gnashing of teeth."[17] It's one or the other—spectacular life everlasting in heaven or everlasting agony in hell. There's no middle ground. The gospel is the only pathway to life. C. S. Lewis states, "In the end that Face which is the delight or the terror of the universe must be turned upon each of us either with one expression or the other, either conferring glory inexpressible or inflicting shame that can never be cured or disguised."[18]

If unbelievers categorically reject the concept of eternal life in either heaven or hell as mere fairy tale or myth (which does nothing to alleviate the fact of it), they can't possibly begin to understand the meaning of their daily labor—or more broadly, the meaning of their vocations. Only in obeying the Master's call, "Come, follow me," do we discover the purpose and meaning of it all, for only then do we begin to see how our labor is swept up

---

[13] Ephesians 2:8–9
[14] Titus 3:5
[15] 2 Timothy 2:12
[16] 2 Thessalonians 1:9
[17] Matthew 13:49–50
[18] Lewis, *The Weight of Glory,* 38.

into his labor—his story, the divine epic of eternity. His story is a story vastly bigger than us.

Unbelievers work but don't truly know why. They may build something, leave a legacy, or support a good cause. But what's the point? If they assume that a person's destiny is death, and that's the end of it, then by definition, they assume that work is ultimately a hideous exercise in futility. Why bother with the effort if we, along with all future generations, are destined to be nothing more than worm food? If humanity's destiny is oblivion, then the meaning of work—even the meaning of life itself—floats aimlessly adrift on a sea of meaningless chance. But in truth, the unbeliever's fate is even worse than oblivion; it is eternal destruction. The unbeliever's fate is hideous indeed unless he or she comes to know the giver of life, the author of vocations.

God's Son, Jesus Christ, bears unspeakable scars that are the work of human hands. Our labor—whether good or evil, whether we are believing or unbelieving—makes a lasting difference in eternity. Any who doubt this truth need only look at the hands, feet, and side of the risen Lord. The glorious body of Jesus Christ will forever bear the scars of nails that were driven by humans. He ascended into heaven, having borne the cosmic weight of our redemption, forever scarred by the price he paid. All the evil of all the ages came hammering down on a single, holy point in time and space; the blood of the infinite flowed through gaping wounds and soaked a manmade cross. We have done our work: we engraved our eternal worth in the body of the Holy One.

Resurrection and transformation do not mean God will eradicate all that people have done to each other or to the Son of God. Resurrection and transformation mean God will make it all pure;

he will transform everything into God-glorifying, everlasting perfection—even what was intended for evil.

God will give no rewards for evil deeds, but he will magnificently transform the wounds inflicted by those deeds. This is a massive source of hope for you and me, because we have done much that is evil. We have wounded others. If you doubt it, just ask the people who've been closest to you throughout your life. There's another reason this truth gives us great hope: many of us have had much evil done to us; we have been wounded and scarred. The gospel heals not only our transgressions, but also our wounds. It transforms them into a glorious wonder. It makes the bearer of the scars more precious, complete, and triumphant than he or she would be without them.

In Romans 8, the apostle Paul gave us one of the most precious promises in all the Bible: "And we know that for those who love God all things work together for good, for those who are called according to his purpose."[19] Do not waver in your hope. *All* things includes *all* things, even scars—even scars borne by the Son of God. Thomas, one of Jesus' twelve disciples, thought all was lost when his Lord was killed on the cross. The other disciples tried to tell him Jesus was risen, but Thomas simply couldn't believe it. *Raised from the dead?* he thought. *Yeah, right.*

> Now Thomas, one of the twelve . . . said to them,
> "Unless I see in his hands the mark of the nails,
> and place my finger into the mark of the nails,
> and place my hand into his side, I will never
> believe." . . . Jesus came and stood among them
> and said, "Peace be with you." Then he said to

[19] Romans 8:28

Thomas, "Put your finger here, and see my hands; and put out your hand, and place it in my side. Do not disbelieve, but believe." Thomas answered him, "My Lord and my God!" (John 20:24–28)

"Before we can begin to see the cross as something done for us, we have to see it as something done by us,"[20] observed John Stott. On the cross, Jesus bore all our sins—yours, mine, and the sins of every person who has ever lived. We murdered the Holy Son of the Most High God. Yet he went to the cross willingly so that he might save us, his murderers. The wonder of the gospel beggars the human mind and annihilates our pride. A. W. Tozer writes, "We must hide our unholiness in the wounds of Christ. . . . We must take refuge from God in God."[21]

"God shows his love for us in that while we were still sinners, Christ died for us. Since, therefore, we have now been justified by his blood, much more shall we be saved by him from the wrath of God."[22] We take refuge in the wounds of Christ not by impressing God with all the work we have done for him, but by joining Thomas and believing in the risen Son, for "whoever believes in the Son has eternal life."[23] We reach out to touch the mark of man-driven nails, and we cry, "My Lord and my God!" Salvation is as simple—and incomprehensible—as that. It's childlike faith; it's infinite mercy.

Jesus saves us, and then he does something more. He bestows on us significance beyond words: he adopts us as his sons and daughters—his heirs. We say a prayer on bended knee, and he re-

---

[20] John R. Stott, *The Cross of Christ* (Downers Grove, IL: InterVarsity, 2006), 63.
[21] A. W. Tozer, *The Knowledge of the Holy* (New York: Harper Collins, 1978), 107.
[22] Romans 5:8–9
[23] John 3:36 (NIV)

sponds by making us, who were formerly his mortal enemies, his beloved children. He removes our hearts of stone and gives us living hearts, hearts that adore him. The "terror of the universe"[24] becomes our loving, all-powerful, infinitely glorious Father. "I will be a father to you, and you shall be sons and daughters to me, says the Lord Almighty."[25] Our response can only be stammering awe.

To the unbeliever, the divine summons is clear: "Come, follow me." Follow Jesus, and he will save you from the horror of eternal destruction. He will liberate your life from the abyss of meaninglessness and despair. You will be able to embrace your vocation, however arduous or unseen it may be, with the echo of the Master's forging hammer ringing in your ears. You can know, beyond all doubt, that he is shaping you for your very own utterly unique, everlasting vocation. The summons of Jesus Christ will carry you and all that you are beyond this vapor of time. It is a summons to life everlasting, beyond the river of death, where the best is yet to come. You, like Mr. Valiant-for-Truth in John Bunyan's *Pilgrim's Progress,* can step to the water's edge knowing it is merely the pathway home to the dwelling place of God with humankind.

> It was noised abroad that Mr. Valiant-for-Truth was taken with a summons. . . . When he understood it, he called for his friends, and told them of it. Then said he, "I am going to my Father's, and though with great difficulty I am got hither, yet now I do not repent me of all the trouble I have been at to arrive where I am. My sword I give to him that shall succeed me in my pilgrimage, and

---

[24] Lewis, *The Weight of Glory,* 38.
[25] 2 Corinthians 6:18

my courage and skill to him that can get it. My marks and scars I carry with me, to be a witness for me, that I have fought his battles, who now will be my Rewarder." When the day that he must go hence, was come, many accompanied him to the river side, into which as he went, he said, *Death, where is thy sting?* And as he went down deeper, he said, *Grave, where is thy victory?* So he passed over, and all the trumpets sounded for him on the other side.[26]

GOD KNOWS YOUR NAME

"There was once a little man called Niggle, who had a long journey to make,"[27] wrote J. R. R. Tolkien in the opening lines of his short fable, *Leaf by Niggle.* Niggle was an inconsequential little painter, unnoticed by the world, whose life ambition was to complete his masterpiece—an exquisitely detailed (and very large) picture of a great tree. He toiled away at his big canvas day after day, year after year. "'At any rate, I shall get this one picture done, my real picture, before I have to go on that wretched journey,' he used to say."[28] The ever-looming journey was the journey we all must someday make—death.

Sensing that his life was fleeting, Niggle rolled up his sleeves and labored at his picture with great intensity. "But there came a tremendous crop of interruptions. Things went wrong in his

---

[26] John Bunyan, *The Pilgrim's Progress: From this World, to That Which is to Come,* ed. Roger Pooley (New York: Penguin, 2009), 311.

[27] J. R. R. Tolkien, "Leaf by Niggle," in *Tree and Leaf: Including Mythopoeia and the Homecoming of Beorhtnoth* (London: HarperCollins, 2001), 93.

[28] Tolkien, *Tree and Leaf,* 95.

house; he had to go and serve on a jury in the town; a distant friend fell ill; Mr Parish [his neighbor] was laid up with lumbago; and visitors kept on coming."[29] In the end, there came one last interruption—a knock on his door. It was the carriage driver; the time for Niggle's long journey had come at last. "'Oh, dear!' said poor Niggle, beginning to weep. 'And it's not even finished!'"[30] His picture was only a shadow of what he had hoped it would be. After he died, the townsfolk used Niggle's big canvas—his life's work, his unfinished masterpiece—to patch the leaky roof on Mr. Parish's house.

Some time later, a schoolmaster found a corner of Niggle's painting "torn off, lying in a field."[31] The schoolmaster "preserved the odd corner. Most of it crumbled; but one beautiful leaf remained intact. . . . He left it to the Town Museum, and for a long while 'Leaf: by Niggle' hung there in a recess, and was noticed by a few eyes. But eventually the Museum was burnt down, and the leaf, and Niggle, were entirely forgotten in his old country."[32]

Tolkien's fable is haunting, because it is what you and I each fear. We quietly suspect that our lives, stripped of all delusions, are really no different than Niggle's. In fact, deep down, we know it's the merciless truth. Our fear—our fate—is to be forgotten. We labor, and we dream. Yet in the end, our work will be unfinished, and our names will be entirely forgotten.

No matter how much you and I accomplish, no matter how famous we are, our work and names will one day vanish. Don't believe it? Quick, without doing a web search, how many Egyptian pharaohs can you name—ten? Two? There were hundreds of them,

29 Tolkien, *Tree and Leaf*, 95–96.
30 Tolkien, *Tree and Leaf*, 102.
31 Tolkien, *Tree and Leaf*, 117.
32 Tolkien, *Tree and Leaf*, 117–118.

spanning three thousand years of pharaonic history. These rulers were so powerful that they were worshiped as gods. How about Persian emperors? They were gods, too. Okay, how about the ten most powerful people who walked on the planet before the year 1,500? The truth is relentless. You and I and our unfinished labor will soon be entirely forgotten. It may take five hundred years or maybe five thousand, but in the grand scheme of things, that's nothing.

The history of humankind is a history of forgotten names. Even the heroic and the wise, as the author of Ecclesiastes tells us, are soon forgotten: "There was a little city with few men in it, and a great king came against it and besieged it, building great siegeworks against it. But there was found in it a poor, wise man, and he by his wisdom delivered the city. Yet no one remembered that poor man."[33]

John Paul Jones, the great naval leader of the American Revolution, stood on a badly damaged sinking ship. The opposing British captain asked for Jones's surrender, but Jones defiantly shouted back, "I have not yet begun to fight." His ensuing victory, against all odds, enshrined Jones as an emblem of the United States Navy. However, you and I would have never heard of John Paul Jones or his famous battle cry (and he wouldn't be entombed today in an elaborate marble and bronze sarcophagus in the US Naval Academy Chapel) if not for a single forgotten sailor.

The ships were locked in rail-to-rail, hand-to-hand combat. During the chaos of the battle, the unknown American sailor, armed with a small handheld bomb, scrambled high into the entangled rigging. He walked the ropes over to the British ship, and

---

[33] Ecclesiastes 9:14–15

from its mast, forty feet up, he lit the fuse of his bomb and
dropped it to the main deck below. It bounced and then fell
through an open hatch to the lower gun-deck, where it landed . . .
in an open barrel of gunpowder. Shortly after Jones issued his defi-
ant battle cry, the little bomb exploded—and so did the entire
gun-deck of the British ship. John Paul Jones had his victory and
his fame. Yet no one remembers the name of the sailor who was
the hero of the battle.[34]

If the names of heroes (people who save entire cities or carry
handheld bombs across the rigging ropes of battling ships) are
soon forgotten, then what chance do you and I have? For every
remembered name, there are countless thousands or even millions
of us who toil our lives away in unheroic labor and then are entirely forgotten. Eventually, even the remembered among us will
all be forgotten, too. Fame is an illusion: five seconds, five years,
five thousand years, then—*poof*—it's gone. You're gone. This is
true unless (and herein lies the great paradox of the gospel) your
fame—*your name*—is anchored in the Son of God, the giver of
everlasting fame. Frederic W. Farrar, English minister and archdea-
con of Westminster Abbey in the late eighteen hundreds, wrote:

> There is a greatness in unknown names, there is an
> immortality of quiet duties, attainable by the
> meanest of human kind; and when the Judge shall
> reverse the tables many of these last shall be
> first. . . . Yes, because they have done their obscure
> duty, their unknown, unnamed, unhonoured, un-
> rewarded duty. . . . To live well in the quiet rou-

---

[34] Ron Carter, *Unlikely Heroes: Ordinary Men and Women Whose Courage Won the Revolution*
(Salt Lake City: Shadow Mountain, 2007), 153–157.

tine of life; to fill a little space because God wills it; to go on cheerfully with a petty round of little duties, little avocations; to accept unmurmuringly a low position; to be misunderstood, misrepresented, maligned, without complaint; to smile for the joys of others when the heart is aching;—to banish all ambition, all pride, and all restlessness, in a single regard to our Savior's work. To do this for a lifetime is a greater effort, and he who does this is a greater hero, than he who for one hour stems a breach, or for one day rushes onward undaunted in the flaming front of shot and shell. His works will follow him. He may not be a hero to the world, but he is one of God's heroes.[35]

God knows your name. There can be no greater fame than to be known and loved by the infinite Lord God Almighty. To have a name that is written down in heaven is to have an everlasting name. Jesus tells us to "rejoice that your names are written in heaven."[36] Those "whose names are in the book of life"[37] will dwell with God forever. If you had to choose, would you choose sixty thousand screaming fans who will forget about you as soon as someone better comes along, or would you choose just one fan— the one who created the other sixty thousand fans and "upholds the universe by the word of his power"?[38] The decision is easy. No audience, no matter how large, is greater than the audience of the one.

[35] Frederic Farrar, *The Fall of Man: And Other Sermons* (London: Macmillan, 1868), 268–270.
[36] Luke 10:20
[37] Philippians 4:3; Revelation 20:15, 21:27
[38] Hebrews 1:3

We are surrounded by a culture of people who, fearing the relentless truth of Niggle's fate, frantically try to create a name for themselves. Yet all the while, Jesus Christ holds out his nail-scarred hands and says, "Come, follow me. I will give you a name, an everlasting name, a spectacularly famous name."

You see, God knows the name you bear today, but he also knows your *other* name—your white-stone name. It's the name that only he and you will ever know; it's your *true* name. "I will give him a white stone, with a new name written on the stone that no one knows except the one who receives it."[39] He gives us our true name—this utter completion of who and what we are—when we bear our battle scars through the river of death and look into the eyes of our mighty captain. "The true name is the one which expresses the character, the nature, the being, the meaning of the person who bears it," writes George MacDonald. "It is the man's own symbol. . . . Who can give a man this, his own name? God alone. For no one but God sees what the man is."[40]

God will make us the marvel we were always meant to be. With the sound of our true name, God will sing the unsung song of our lives. He will complete us. He will take the most unlikely, regular, everyday, forgotten people and make us immortal heirs of the universe. We will at last know the unutterable depths of God's decree: "Fear not, for I have redeemed you; I have called you by name, you are mine."[41]

On that river-crossing day, all the things we've experienced in life will suddenly make sense. It turns out that our white-stone name has been our true name all along. It's the person God had in

[39] Revelation 2:17
[40] George MacDonald, *Unspoken Sermons, Series I, II & III* (Whitehorn, CA: Johannesen, 1997), 71.
[41] Isaiah 43:1

mind when he created us—the person he's shaped us to be through all the battles, trials, wounds, labors, blessings, and victories of life. We press forward in the battle all the way to the river's edge. Yet, on this side, in this fallen world, our lives remain unfinished, unsung, and unbuilt.[42] The day will come, however, when he will tell us our name. And as MacDonald writes, "To tell the name, is to seal the success—to say, 'In thee also I am well pleased.'"[43]

COMPLETED BUT NOT FINISHED

We will each become our true name, spectacularly transformed, completed, and made perfect—*but not finished.* To be transformed, completed, and made perfect does not mean we are finished in the sense that nothing more can be added to us or changed. God is infinite. His glory is infinite. You and I are not infinite. We never will be—not even in heaven. God is all-knowing, all-powerful, omnipresent, and sovereign. We'll never be any of those things— not even close. We will have room to grow, learn, and behold new things. Heaven isn't the end of the line. It isn't a place where we are stuck in a never-changing, blissfully finished state of existence, never again to explore, create, or flourish. John Piper writes, "Heaven will be a never-ending, ever-increasing discovery of more and more of God's glory with greater and ever-greater joy in him."[44]

---

42 Philippians 3:12–21
43 MacDonald, *Unspoken Sermons,* 72.
44 John Piper, *God's Passion for His Glory: Living in the Vision of Jonathan Edwards* (Wheaton, IL: Crossway, 2006), 37.

Heaven isn't the end of the story. It is, rather, just the beginning. This life is our apprenticeship. Through it all, God is training you and me for the task ahead. He's equipping us with unique abilities, interests, and insights. He's preparing us for the everlasting adventure—and what an adventure it will be! C. S. Lewis concludes his great epic, *The Chronicles of Narnia,* with a spellbinding image of our destiny. After all the battles and trials of life, after countless peaks of soaring joy and many valleys of deep despair, the end comes at last. Life is over; the young kings and queens of Narnia are killed in a railway accident.

> But for them it was only the beginning of the real story. All their life in this world and all their adventures in Narnia had only been the cover and the title page: now at last they were beginning Chapter One of the Great Story which no one on earth has read: which goes on forever: in which every chapter is better than the one before.[45]

The earth was perfect and complete when God created it, but it wasn't finished. Adam and Eve were perfect and complete before the fall of humankind, but they weren't finished. They weren't all-knowing, all-powerful beings. Instead, they were limited and finite, and they had work to do—a mandate to fulfill. They were perfectly and completely equipped for the task ahead. There was exploring to be done, lands to discover, and mountains to climb. There was an earth to rule over, tend, subdue, and fill. The human race is an ever-progressing race not because of sin or the fall, but because God made it so before the fall. He hard-wired us to ex-

---

45 Lewis, *The Last Battle,* 210–211.

plore, learn, grow, flourish, and rule. These activities are integral parts of our being created in his image. They are a reflection of his glory.

The Bible begins and ends with creation. In the opening pages of Genesis, God creates the earth. In the closing pages of Revelation, God recreates the earth—the new earth. You and I will be restored to humankind's original role and task—our adventure, the great story. In heaven, there will be exploring to be done, lands to discover, and mountains to climb. There will be a new earth to rule. We will have work to do.

Day by day, we will behold more and more of God's glory. We'll never reach the end of it, for it has no end. Heaven is more than we've imagined; it's the unified new earth and new heavens.[46] Heaven is a new *universe*—an unspeakably beautiful outpouring of God's wisdom, glory, and grace. Equipped with spectacularly powerful gifts, bodies, and minds, you and I will forever explore and reign over the vast reaches of a universe that is incomprehensibly more stunning than it is today. This is why the apostle Paul, facing torture and execution, could say, "I consider that the sufferings of this present time are not worth comparing with the glory that is to be revealed to us."[47] God's glory is infinite. Our destiny is to behold it forever. All the while, his Son, Jesus Christ, will reign with us as our Savior, King, and our guide. Oh, the wonder of it!

> When I look at your heavens, the work of your fingers,
> the moon and the stars, which you have set in place,
> what is man that you are mindful of him,
> and the son of man that you care for him?

---

[46] Isaiah 65:17, 66:22; 2 Peter 3:13; Revelation 21:1
[47] Romans 8:18

> Yet you have made him a little lower than the heavenly beings
> and crowned him with glory and honor.
> You have given him dominion over the works of your hands;
> you have put all things under his feet. (Psalm 8:3–6)

In the end, there will come one last interruption to our lives—a knock on our door. The time for our long journey will come at last. When we cross the river and our feet touch the far shore, we'll discover something quite amazing and unexpected, yet familiar. Our unfinished labor will be wondrously completed and made perfect, but not finished. Our adventure isn't over; it's only just begun. You and I have work to do—and so does Niggle.

EQUIPPED FOR THE ADVENTURE

"The birds were building in the Tree. Astonishing birds: how they sang!"[48] Upon reaching heaven, Niggle discovered the most extraordinary surprise: "Before him stood the Tree, his Tree,"[49] alive and real! It was more real than he had ever imagined it could be, "its leaves opening, its branches growing and bending in the wind."[50] His labor was wondrously transformed and completed. God touched it with the infinite power of his glory.

As Niggle gazed at the tree in bewilderment, something more struck him: the forests and mountains—brushstrokes he'd painted merely to fill the empty spaces beyond the tree—all became real, too! At first, of course, Niggle was overcome with the wonder of it all, but he gradually realized, as Tolkien put it, "The Tree was fin-

---

[48] Tolkien, *Tree and Leaf,* 110.
[49] Tolkien, *Tree and Leaf,* 109.
[50] Tolkien, *Tree and Leaf,* 109–110.

ished, though not finished . . . in the Forest there were a number of inconclusive regions, that still needed work and thought. Nothing needed altering any longer, nothing was wrong, as far as it had gone, but it needed continuing."[51] Niggle still had work to do—exhilarating work.

Niggle stumbled into his old neighbor, Mr. Parish, who had always loved gardening. Together, they set about the marvelous task before them. They tended, managed, nurtured, and created. "Niggle would think of wonderful new flowers and plants, and Parish always knew exactly where to set them and where they would do best."[52] They worked, and they explored in fathomless joy, ever learning, ever beholding the glory of it all.

God created us to create—not just until we're sixty-five, but forever. Your divine biography doesn't end with death, and it doesn't turn into an interminably boring routine in heaven. Little fairy wings, a harp, fluffy clouds, choir practice forever and ever? Nope! There's a redeemed universe to tend, manage, and nurture. There are new marvels to create. You and I will be God's image-bearers for all eternity. He is the master craftsman, the worker, the Creator of it all. Yet we will magnify his glory and bear his image, in part, by working. Rudyard Kipling put it this way: "The Master of all good workmen shall put us to work anew."[53]

God rewards his sons and daughters with levels of responsibility. He gives them tasks to do. Upon reaching heaven, they'll hear the Master say, "Well done, good and faithful servant. You have been faithful over a little; I will set you over much. Enter into the joy of your master."[54] "The Lord God will be their light, and they

---

[51] Tolkien, *Tree and Leaf*, 111.
[52] Tolkien, *Tree and Leaf*, 113.
[53] Rudyard Kipling, *The Complete Verse* (London: Kyle Cathie, 2006), 181.
[54] Matthew 25:23

will reign forever and ever."[55] Reigning over the new earth or being "set over much" implies activity—a task to do. It does not imply receiving an empty title of eminence in which the supposed ruler has nothing to actually rule.

Like Adam and Eve before the fall, you and I will once again work for the sheer, worshipful joy of it. Life, work, and worship will all be one. We'll work because it's a radiant outpouring of our God-given gifts—gifts that billions of us have never had the chance to use or even discover in this fallen world.

In heaven, every single person will at last have the freedom to work in the center of his or her unleashed gifts. Each of us will have a role to fill—our task, our story. Each of us will be spectacularly equipped for the adventure that lies before us. The vast array of gifts in the body of Christ will blaze forth, each a priceless, essential facet of the diamond. "The work on the other side, whatever be its character, will be adapted to each one's special aptitudes and powers," wrote James Campbell. "It will be the work he can do best; the work that will give the fullest play to all that is within him."[56] The career coach's statement was absolutely true: "God never wastes our gifts, and he plans to use them for his glory." The only question was, *When?* The answer, it turns out, is *forever.*

YOU HAVE A ROLE IN THE STORY

The day will come when we will each see the giver of our gifts face to face. On that day, we will at last fully know that, all along, our biographies were secure in the sovereign hand of God. He was

[55] Revelation 22:5
[56] James Campbell, *Heaven Opened: A Book of Comfort and Hope* (New York: Fleming H. Revell, 1924), 123.

preparing us for our role in the great story—his story. As James Campbell neared the end of his life, which he had spent laboring as both a pastor and an author, he wrote:

> No preparation is ever in vain. . . . If some kinds of work are over, others will begin; if some duties are laid down, others will be taken up. And any regret for labour missed down here, will be swallowed up in joyful anticipation of the higher service that awaits every prepared and willing worker in the upper kingdom of the Father.[57]

Grace, the Egyptian fallahin peasant, has a role in the story. Haitian immigrant taxicab drivers have a role in the story. Thousands of young soldiers who died on the battlefield, their gifts and dreams not yet realized, have a role in the story. The countless billions who endured lives of peasant toil, all the forgotten names in history of people who never had the opportunity to display their God-given gifts—each has a unique, everlasting role in God's story. And so do you.

No matter how obscure our lives may seem today, we will one day radiate the glory of God before redeemed humankind and all the mighty hosts of heaven. No one will be forgotten, ignored, or belittled as insignificant to God. Like the one-of-a-kind stars above, each of us, crafted by a lifetime of experiences, will reflect our one-of-a-kind aspect of the divine glory. "For star differs from star in glory. So is it with the resurrection of the dead."[58] The Maker of stars is the Maker of you and me. He is our Father and

---

[57] Campbell, *Heaven Opened,* 124.
[58] 1 Corinthians 15:41–42

our God. "Lift your eyes and look to the heavens: Who created all these? He who brings out the starry host one by one, and calls them each by name. Because of his great power and mighty strength, not one of them is missing."[59]

We've seen a great paradox here. The blood of Jesus Christ alone purchased our significance to God. Our vocations are entirely incapable of purchasing our eternal worth. Yet, all along, God has equipped us for the magnificent adventure of eternity in part through the experiences of our work, roles, and relationships—our everyday, earthly vocations.

Many people live in quiet despair over the seeming insignificance of their lives. They wonder if all the toil—the daily grind of life—is totally meaningless in the grand scheme of things. People just like you and me quietly ache with a vague, hollow fear—a sense that all the exhausting effort it takes to live this life will leave no lasting fingerprint on eternity. But the Bible shows us that the daily grind of our lives is striking cosmic hammer-blows that forge the very shape of eternity!

God is forging his masterpiece with our random-arrow lives. He's given each of us a unique life to live—a particular place to strike the white-hot ingot of eternity. We each have our very own place in his story. Like master to apprentice, he entrusts the hammer to our hands. He says, "Strike it. Strike it right here. This is your place. This is where I want you to shape eternity. Live the life I gave you to live." In stammering awe, we take up the hammer. We live our regular, everyday lives. The hammer falls. Sparks fly, and the Master, our Father, is delighted.

---

59 Isaiah 40:26 (NIV)

Our journey together in this book began by exposing the lie of vocational guilt. Now we have seen the Truth—his name is Jesus. He is the source and giver of our significance. He gave us the answer to our question; he wrote it with his blood. Our undiscovered gifts, our unapplauded work, our forgotten names, and our unsung lives all matter. *They matter to God.* They'll be part of his masterpiece—and oh, what an astonishing, breathtaking wonder it will be! Jesus Christ, the Holy Son of the Most High God, the one whose name is above all names, died for you, and he died for me. With the blood-soaked cry, "It is finished," he redeemed our lives and our worth for all eternity. "Therefore God has highly exalted him and bestowed on him the name that is above every name, so that at the name of Jesus every knee should bow, in heaven and on earth and under the earth, and every tongue confess that Jesus Christ is Lord, to the glory of God the Father."[60]

---

[60] Philippians 2:9–11

WORKS CITED

Aburdene, Patricia. *Megatrends 2010: The Rise of Conscious Capitalism.* Charlottesville, VA: Hampton Roads, 2007.

Adams, Scott. *14 Years of Loyal Service in a Fabric-Covered Box.* Kansas City: Andrews McMeel, 2009.

Alcorn, Randy. *Heaven.* Carol Stream, IL: Tyndale House, 2004.

————. *The Treasure Principle.* Colorado Springs: Multnomah, 2001.

Banks, Robert J. *Faith Goes to Work: Reflections from the Marketplace.* Eugene, OR: Wipf and Stock, 1999.

BBC News. "Oprah 'Most Powerful Celebrity.'" June 14, 2007. http://news.bbc.co.uk/2/hi/entertainment/6753847.stm.

Bradford, Ernle. *Thermopylae: The Battle for the West.* Cambridge, MA: Da Capo Press, 2004.

Bunyan, John. *The Pilgrim's Progress: From this World, to That Which is to Come.* Edited by Roger Pooley. New York: Penguin, 2009.

Bushnell, Horace. *Sermons for the New Life.* New York: Charles Scribner's Sons, 1904.

Byrne, John A. "The Promise of Reinvention." *Fast Company,* August 1, 2003. www.fastcompany.com/magazine/73/edlet.html.

Calvin, John. *Commentary on a Harmony of the Evangelists, Matthew, Mark, and Luke, Vol. 2.* Translated by William Pringle. Edinburgh, Scotland: Calvin Translation Society, 1845.

Campbell, James. *Heaven Opened: A Book of Comfort and Hope.* New York: Fleming H. Revell, 1924.

Carter, Ron. *Unlikely Heroes: Ordinary Men and Women Whose Courage Won the Revolution.* Salt Lake City: Shadow Mountain, 2007.

Chambers, Oswald. *My Utmost For His Highest.* Uhrichsville, OH: Barbour and Company, 1987.

Chesterton, G. K. *Orthodoxy.* Chicago: Moody, 2009.

Da Vinci, Leonardo. *Thoughts on Art and Life.* Translated by Maurice Baring. Boston: Merrymount Press, 1906.

Dearlove, Des. "The Workplace Gets Spiritual." *The Times of London,* July 24, 2003. http://business.timesonline.co.uk/tol/business/career_and_jobs/graduate_management/article847676.ece.

Diehl, William E. *Christianity and Real Life.* Philadelphia: Fortress, 1976.

Duckat, Walter. *Beggar to King: All the Occupations of Biblical Times.* Garden City, NY: Doubleday and Company, 1968.

Farrar, Frederic. *The Fall of Man: And Other Sermons.* London: Macmillan, 1868.

Fischer, Steven Rogers. *A History of Writing.* London: Reaktion Books, 2003.

Gibbs, Nancy. "How America Has Run Out of Time." *Time,* April 24, 1989. www.time.com/time/magazine/article/0,9171,957505-2,00.html.

Gladwell, Malcolm. *Outliers: The Story of Success.* New York: Little, Brown and Company, 2008.

Golding, William. "The Hot Gates." *The Sparta Pages.* http://uts.cc.utexas.edu/~sparta/topics/essays/academic/golding.htm.

Greene, Mark. *The Great Divide.* London: LICC, 2010.

Guinness, Os. *The Call: Finding and Fulfilling the Central Purpose of Your Life.* Nashville, TN: Thomas Nelson, 2003.

Hardy, Lee. *The Fabric of This World: Inquiries Into Calling, Career Choice, and the Design of Human Work.* Grand Rapids: William B. Eerdmans, 1990.

Heimler, Eugene. *Mental Illness and Social Work.* Harmondsworth, Middlesex, England: Penguin Books, 1967.

Henry, Matthew. *Matthew Henry's Commentary on the Whole Bible: Complete and Unabridged in One Volume.* Peabody, MA: Hendrickson, 1991. *Logos Bible Software.* Bellingham, WA: Logos, 2009.

Herbermann, Charles G., ed., et al. *The Catholic Encyclopedia: An International Work of Reference on the Constitution, Doctrine, Discipline, and History of the Catholic Church.* Vol. 5. New York: Robert Appleton, 1909.

Josephus, Flavius. *The Antiquities of the Jews.* In *Josephus: Complete Works,* translated by William Whiston. Grand Rapids: Kregel, 1966.

Keller, Helen. *The Open Door.* Garden City, NY: Doubleday, 1957.

Kipling, Rudyard. *The Complete Verse.* With foreword by M. M. Kaye. London: Kyle Cathie, 2006.

Lencioni, Patrick. *The Three Signs of a Miserable Job.* San Francisco: Jossey-Bass, 2007.

Lewis, C. S. *The Discarded Image: An Introduction to Medieval and Renaissance Literature.* Canto ed. New York: Cambridge University Press, 1994.

———. *The Horse and His Boy.* New York: HarperCollins, 1994.

———. *The Last Battle.* New York: HarperCollins, 1994.

———. *Letters to Malcolm: Chiefly on Prayer.* San Diego: Harcourt, 2002.

———. *The Problem of Pain.* San Francisco: HarperCollins, 2001.

———. *The Weight of Glory: And Other Addresses.* New York: HarperCollins, 2001.

Luther, Martin. "The Babylonian Captivity of the Church." In *Three Treatises,* translated and revised by A. T. W. Steinhäuser, et al. Philadelphia: Fortress Press, 1970.

——. "An Open Letter to the Christian Nobility of the German Nation Concerning the Reform of the Christian Estate." In *Callings: Twenty Centuries of Christian Wisdom on Vocation,* edited by William C. Placher. Grand Rapids: William B. Eerdmans, 2005.

——. "Whether Soldiers, Too, Can Be Saved." In *Callings: Twenty Centuries of Christian Wisdom on Vocation,* edited by William C. Placher. Grand Rapids: William B. Eerdmans, 2005.

Lynes, Russell. "Time on Our Hands." *Harpers,* July 1958, 34.

MacDonald, Charles B., and Martin Blumenson. "Defeat of Germany." In *A Concise History of World War II,* edited by Vincent J. Esposito. New York: Frederick A. Praeger, 1964.

Macdonald, George. *Unspoken Sermons, Series I, II and III.* Whitehorn, CA: Johannesen, 1997.

MacLeod, George. *Only One Way Left.* Glasgow: Wild Goose Publications, 1956.

Maloof, Rich. "Monday Morning Heart Attacks . . . and Other Health Risks by the Day of the Week." *MSN Health and Fitness,* February 24, 2011. http://health.msn.com/health-topics/monday-morning-heart-attacks-and-other-health-risks-by-the-day-of-the-week.

Meigs, Robert F., and Walter B. Meigs. *Accounting: The Basis for Business Decisions.* New York: McGraw-Hill, 1990.

Miller, Darrow L., with Marit Newton. *LifeWork: A Biblical Theology for What You Do Every Day.* Seattle: YWAM, 2009.

Miller, David W. *God at Work: The History and Promise of the Faith at Work Movement.* New York: Oxford University Press, 2007.

MSNBC.com. "Americans Hate Their Jobs More Than Ever." February 26, 2007.http://www.msnbc.msn.com/id/17348695/ns/business-careers/t/americans-hate-their-jobs-more-ever/.

Nash, Laura, and Scotty McLennan. *Church on Sunday, Work on Monday: The Challenge of Fusing Christian Values with Business Life.* San Francisco: Jossey-Bass, 2001.

Novak, Michael. *Business as a Calling: Work and the Examined Life.* New York: Free Press, 1996.

Orthodox Presbyterian Church. *The Westminster Confession of Faith and Catechisms: with Proof Texts.* Lawrenceville, GA: The Christian Education and Publications Committee of the Presbyterian Church in America, 2005.

Piper, John. *Desiring God: Meditations of a Christian Hedonist.* Sisters, OR: Multnomah, 1996.

———. *Don't Waste Your Life.* Wheaton, IL: Crossway, 2004.

———. *Future Grace: The Purifying Power of Living by Faith in Future Grace.* New York: Multnomah, 1995.

———. *God's Passion for His Glory: Living the Vision of Jonathan Edwards.* Wheaton, IL: Crossway, 2006.

———. "What Is the Will of God and How Do We Know It?" Sermon, August 22, 2004.http://www.desiringgod.org/resource-library/ sermons/what-is-the-will-of-god-and-how-do-we-know-it.

Sayers, Dorothy L. "Vocation in Work." In *A Christian Basis for the Post-War World,* edited by Albert E. Baker. London: Student Christian Movement Press, 1942.

Schaeffer, Francis A. *The Finished Work of Christ: The Truth of Romans 1–8.* Wheaton, IL: Crossway, 1998.

———. *No Little People.* Wheaton, IL: Crossway, 2003.

Schor, Juliet B. *The Overworked American: The Unexpected Decline of Leisure.* New York: Basic Books, 1993.

Snyder, Zack, Frank Miller, Kurt Johnstad, Lynn Varley, and Michael Gordon, Screenwriters. *300.* DVD. Directed by Zack Snyder. Warner Home Video, 2007.

Stevens, Paul R. *Doing God's Business: Meaning and Motivation for the Marketplace.* Grand Rapids: William B. Eerdmans, 2006.

————, and Robert Banks, eds. *The Marketplace Ministry Handbook: A Manual for Work, Money and Business.* Vancouver: Regent College, 2005.

Stott, John R. *The Cross of Christ.* Downers Grove, IL: InterVarsity, 2006.

Sullivan, Robert, ed. *LIFE 100 People Who Changed the World.* New York: Life Books, 2010.

Tamny, John. "Embrace the Wealth Gap." *The American Spectator,* May 8, 2007. http://spectator.org/archives/2007/05/08/embrace-the- wealth-gap#.

Taylor, LaTonya. "The Church of O." *Christianity Today,* April 1, 2002. http://www.christianitytoday.com/ct/2002/april1/1.38.html?start=2.

Terkel, Studs. *Working: People Talk about What They Do All Day and How They Feel about What They Do.* New York: New Press, 1997.

Time.com. "Global Influentials: The Top 25 Business People Worldwide." December 2001. http://www.time.com/time/2001/influentials/.

Tolkien, J. R. R. *The Lord of the Rings.* New York: Houghton Mifflin, 1994.

————. "Leaf by Niggle." In *Tree and Leaf: Including Mythopoeia and the Homecoming of Beorhtnoth.* London: HarperCollins, 2001.

Tozer, A. W. *The Knowledge of the Holy.* New York: HarperCollins, 1978.

————. *The Pursuit of God.* Camp Hill, PA: Christian Publications, 1993.

Twain, Mark. *The Autobiography of Mark Twain*. New York: HarperCollins, 2000.

US Bureau of Labor Statistics. Compensation and Working Conditions. *Wages in the Nonprofit Sector: Management, Professional, and Administrative Support Occupations,* by Amy Butler (April 15, 2009). http://www.bls.gov/opub/cwc/cm20081022 ar01p1.htm.

———. *Occupational Outlook Handbook,* last modified March 29, 2012. http://www.bls.gov/ooh.

———. *Standard Occupational Classification,* last modified March 11, 2010. http://www.bls.gov/soc/2010/soc530000.htm.

Warren, Rick. *The Purpose Driven Life: What On Earth Am I Here For?* Grand Rapids: Zondervan, 2002.

Wingren, Gustaf. *Luther on Vocation.* Translated by Carl C. Rasmussen. Eugene, OR: Wipf and Stock, 2004.

Yancey, Philip. "Living with Furious Opposites." *Christianity Today,* September 4, 2000. www.christianitytoday.com/ct/2000/september 4/4.70.html.

SCRIPTURE INDEX